MY MOTHER'S DAUGHTER
A Life in Stories

NANCY McKEEVER

Copyright © 2024 Nancy McKeever

All rights reserved, including the reproduction in whole or in any part in any form without the written consent of the author.

ISBN 978-1-959457-26-8

Published in the United States by
Blue Jay Ink

FOREWORD

I consider myself a very lucky person for the day Nancy McKeever stepped into my memoir writing course at Santa Monica College's Emeritus Program. Each time she shared a story, her fellow classmates and I held our collective breath because we knew we were in for a treat. Her stories were so vivid and rich in detail, and the people she wrote about, particularly her mother, seemed to come to life before our eyes. It was not an easy life she was writing about—the family struggled for basic necessities in one of the poorest neighborhoods of Pittsburgh, Pennsylvania—and yet even a story about the weekly killing of bedbugs, or the torturous straightening of hair of the four sisters, was told with such honesty, warmth, and humor that we listeners felt let into a world of love and care. Nancy's talents as a writer were apparent early on, and as she continued to write, more and more stories emerged of her remarkable life.

The power of memoir is that it gives us the lived life. The best memoirs allow us to step into someone else's shoes, and when we do, our eyes are opened to whole new realities. Statistics and journalistic accounts, or even the best books on race in America, cannot transport us into a home where a self-taught woman, raised in the rural South, nurtures her six children by reciting poetry and inspires them to pursue their own passions and interests, to prevail over racism and bigotry. Nancy's book reminds us of the importance of the individual story. As we immerse ourselves in these stories, we feel deeply touched by the power of familial love. Even more so, over the course of the book, we get to watch her build a career and fashion a unique life, often out of hardship, but always with deep optimism and an open-minded spirit that allows her to extend the traditional definitions of family and love. She is truly a modern woman, forging her own ideas and practices that should serve as a model for all of us.

It has been a great privilege and honor to know Nancy, and to work with her on getting this book out into the world. It deserves a wide audience so that many others can come to cherish these extraordinary stories of a life lived with honesty, courage, and yes, love.

Monona Wali

PROLOGUE

As I age, I often find myself reflecting on events—both good and not so good—that occurred during my childhood. I used to think of my life as common, or even boring. But in review, I now feel this is untrue. Nothing can be boring in a household that reveals the ups and downs of a family consisting of six children, an absentee father, and one remarkable mother. A mother who somehow, under the most difficult circumstances, made each of her children feel loved, wanted, and special. I don't know how she did this, but she did, and many squabbles occurred because of one sibling teasing another about this point. Here's an example:

Child number one: "See, I told you Momma loved me best."

Child number two: "Why do you say that?"

Child number one: "Because, look, she gave me the biggest pancake!"

Child number two: "Momma!" (Usually followed by raised voices and/or loud crying.)

From this exchange, we would be off and running, each of us listing the "proof" that showed which one was truly her favorite. This exchange never lasted long, however, because deep in our heart of hearts, each of us knew we were truly the best of her children.

Thinking about this now makes me smile still, ever secure in the knowledge that I was the favored one. Reviewing our lives together, I think of her as a magician. How else can you account for the fact that on her very tight budget she still managed to scrape together the ingredients for a birthday cake for each of her children? Or how on her shoestring (a very generous use of the word) budget she managed to afford the 25 cents to allow each of her children to attend the movie theater—22 cents for admission and the pooling together of the remaining monies to buy snacks? She did all this while cleaning other people's homes and getting very little support from our father.

I wrote these stories over the course of eight years to try to capture not only who she was but also to understand the life I was able to create out of that childhood of growing up poor and Black in 1940s Pittsburgh. Some of the stories I have never told before, secrets that I thought would be buried with me. Some of the stories may surprise you for the unexpected turns in my life. I wrote them out of a deep love for my siblings, and others in my life who became extended families, and for my two daughters so they could know the life I experienced. Writing them helped me see how I truly am my mother's daughter. I think of her often and hope that I have managed to convey at least some of the intrinsic traits that made her who she was.

My Mother's Daughter

Nancy J. McKeever

CONTENTS

BEGINNINGS
Homecoming 12
Perfect 18
A Summons to the Principal's Office 23

SUSIE
The Wordsmith 30
Overpaid 35
Purple Memory 40

FAMILY LIFE
The Candy Man 50
Crowning Glory 58
A Family Affair 64
My Billy 68
Dancing Queen 73
The Drummer 79
Look Toward the Future 84
The Price of Silence 90

NURSE NANCY
The Postman 112
Big Girls Don't Cry 117
The Kiss That Stopped Traffic 123
Donald 129
Full Circle 137

MAKING A LIFE
True Confession 144
From Friend to Family 150
Swimming Lessons 157
Momma Was Right 163

GOING HOME
NO REGRETS 172
NO FOOL, NO FUN 178
TRY A LITTLE TENDERNESS 186

MOVING ON
LOST IN TRANSLATION 196
WHAT HAPPENS IN VEGAS... 201
EVERY PICTURE TELLS A STORY 209
INVICTUS 217
AND THEN THERE WERE THREE 224
SWEET POTATO PIE 232
YAY PARADE 238
FLYING 245
THE GIFTS OF MUSIC 251
A GENTLE TOUCH OF MEMORY 258

SPEAKING OF RACE
LIKE A FLY IN BUTTERMILK 268
THE COLOR OF FRIENDSHIP 273
BELIEVE 280
JACKASSERY 286

GOODBYE SUE
BEFORE I'M GONE 294
GOODBYE SUE 300
ACCEPTANCE 306

Susie, Billy, Snip, Chuckie, Nancy, Mimsi, Judy

Snip, Chuckie, Susie, Nancy, Mimsi, Judy

BEGINNINGS

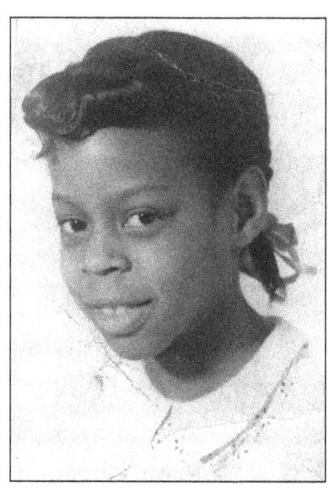

Homecoming

I would lie with my eyes tightly closed and try to imagine what was going on at home without me. I'd picture my mother and brothers and sisters sitting around the small white drop-leaf enamel table eating dinner. Home was a sagging, shabby brick and wooden tenement building. So different from the old dollhouse that we used to play with, and in which we wished we lived. Six, and sometimes, when my father was there, seven people squeezed into a tiny two-room apartment. The kitchen served as a bedroom at night for five-year-old Chuckie and twelve-year-old Billy, who slept head to foot in a rollaway bed. This was stored in the corner during the day. And then there was a bedroom where the other five of us slept. My mother and father shared a double bed. One-year-old Judy slept in a small crib hugging my parents' bed so closely that it looked like one solid piece of furniture that you could only exit from one side.

I, all of three years old, shared a single bed with my ten-year-old sister, Shirley, or Snip, as she was called. Positioned on the far side of this same room, the bed was crammed tightly against one cracked plaster wall, the foot pressing up against a small window, also allowing an exit from only one side. Only room for the bare necessities, but it was home and I was not there.

I was in Pittsburgh Hospital on the Pediatric service. I had been taken there after a week of fever, coughing, and general malaise. I had whooping cough. It was the early 1940s, and while work was being completed on vaccines for this highly infectious disease that killed thousands of children each year, it was not yet under control. Once we arrived at the hospital and the diagnosis was made, my mother was told that I would be hospitalized and quarantined for two weeks. Not only was she not taking me home with her, she also could not visit for fear that she could infect one of the other children who inhabited that small space we called home. What I remember her saying was "Momma has to leave now. You be a big girl and don't cry. Remember, Momma loves you."

She told me, when we talked about this when I was an adult, that she didn't know how to explain what was happening to me. She went on to say that although she told me not to cry, she sat on the trolley sobbing quietly after she left the hospital.

This statement, "Remember, Momma loves you," was the way she ended every telephone conversation I had with her for the rest of my life.

I had no idea how long I was hospitalized. At the time, it seemed as if my mother had been gone forever.

Apparently, it was a little over two weeks, but my three-year-old sense of time distorted the passing hours. I recall the crib where I was placed, which looked like a regular crib but then had an additional covering on the top so that it resembled a large cage. I suppose it was constructed that way so children could not accidentally crawl out over the side. It didn't feel claustrophobic, and since I was being a "good girl," I was never tempted to try to crawl out. Because I wasn't used to sleeping alone at night, my body would automatically seek the presence of another, so that by morning I would have moved all the way to the back side of the crib with my body pressed tightly against the wooden bars. Forgotten were the memories of Snip and I fighting over the skimpy covers. Those memories were replaced by the times that she would tell me stories or hold me close when the apartment was cold. I wanted to be home! I don't remember seeing any other children, only hearing crying once in a while, which helped to remind me that I was not the only child there. Always the compliant one, I tried to remain quietly in bed listening to all the sounds. I could hear the murmur of voices, the crying of other children, and the light, rapid footsteps of the various nurses as they moved up and down the hall. The steps of the physicians would sound heavier and slower, as if they were giving the nurses time to prepare things before their arrival. I would hear other footsteps and wonder, "Is that Momma?" Sometimes it was a nurse with food or medication, but never my mother or any familiar face. Never a Black face.

"I want my Momma," I'd say to the nurses.

"Your mother will come for you when you're well."

I wanted to cry but tried hard not to, as my mother had asked.

One nurse said, "Lie on your stomach, think of your mommy, and try to relax."

I tried this more than once, but it never seemed to help. It just seemed to make my stomach ache even more and the wish to be home even stronger. At no time did I ever think my mother wouldn't come for me. I just wondered when.

After many days, a nurse came into the room and said, "Nancy, you're going home tomorrow, so we're going to put you in the bathtub today." Finally, I was going home. Two nurses placed me in a huge bathtub to bathe me. They washed my hair, and even at three years old, I knew what that meant, but no matter; tomorrow I would be home, and Momma would fix it. As a Black female, I knew that after the shampoo, my mother would then have to "straighten" my hair, a task that required patience from both my mother and me, but at least this arduous task could be completed at home with me tucked comfortably between Momma's thighs.

The next morning, I sat waiting eagerly for my mother to bring clothes for me to wear home. I heard footsteps in the hall. They slowed as they reached my door and I waited, holding my breath and wondering, is it her? Into the room, with a big smile on her face, walked my Aunt Clara. She was my mother's favorite sister and our favorite aunt.

Picking me up and hugging me tightly, she said, "Your mother had to work today, so I'm taking you home. Oh my goodness, they washed your hair! Well, your mother will straighten it when you're stronger."

"Will Momma be mad, Aunt Clara?"

"No baby, your Momma just wants you home."

I suppose she had to sign papers or do something to prove I was hers to take, but the next thing I remember is sitting in the front seat of my Uncle Johnny's battered old truck, which he sometimes used to take us to the County Fair. All the cousins would pile into the back of the old pickup, wave at passers-by, and wait to go through the Liberty Tubes, whose fluorescent lights made everyone's skin have a green-tinged glow.

"Ready to go home, little girl?" he said in his loud but loving voice. "Everyone is waiting for you."

As we rounded the corner of Oakwood Street from Frankstown Avenue, I could barely sit still. Stopping in front of the building, I looked up and for the first time it actually looked good to me. I was glad to see the old building leaning slightly to one side. Glad to climb those oiled, wooden stairs, slightly sunken in the middle, making it necessary to stretch my skinny three-year-old legs to insure I could navigate the uneven surface of the worn stairs. Glad to walk down the narrow, dark hall and reach the last door on the left, where the door opened before I even knocked. They were all there. Well, not my father, but my mother having just arrived and still taking off her coat, my brothers and sisters and even my Aunt Sarah, whose apartment adjoined ours. All smiling and hugging me. Letting me know that while our home looked nothing like the dollhouse, it was a place where I was wanted and loved and belonged.

"Oh Momma, I'm so glad to be home," I cried, tears streaming down my face.

"I'm glad you're home too, baby, 'cause you're Momma's good girl." She was crying also.

Two of my sisters said, "Look Momma, they washed her hair!"

"It's only hair, girls. Your sister's home."

Perfect

I awakened in my crib and fully extended my thin, cramped legs by maneuvering my feet between its bars. I must have been approximately five years old. I had slept in the crib far longer than was appropriate for a child of my size. I didn't fit, and this not fitting in was reflected in my general feeling about my place in the household. In reality, there truly wasn't adequate space of any kind in that cramped two-room cold-water tenement that I shared with the other seven members of my family.

For starters, I was the middle child of seven (although one of my brothers died at just eleven months old, right before my fifth birthday). I looked nothing like my other siblings. They would tease me, as siblings do, and tell me I was adopted, and even though I didn't really believe them, it still made me feel like I didn't quite belong. All of my brothers and sisters' skin ranged from an earthy brown color with a rich tint of a red glow to darker shades. And me, where did I fit in with all this chocolate perfection that I saw in everyone else? I was tall for my age, and skinny. My skin tone was what my Aunt Sarah used to call "high yella," and I had rusty, reddish-brown hair. I was very near-sighted and so flat-footed that my father's sister had to buy the first pair of orthopedic shoes for me as a child since my parents couldn't afford them. The final insult was that I was a sickly child, and in those tight quarters, this could spell disaster. If one child had the measles, everyone soon had them. My siblings would become ill, recover, and then be back up and active, and I would still have a lingering fever or some unexplained complication from even the most common childhood ailment. Complications, of course, resulted in added expenses, which only placed additional strain on our meager resources. I remember clearly when my father made one of his unpredictable "visits" home. At that time, he was still dividing his presence between our family and a second family. Invariably, he would arrive like a blustering tornado, upsetting routines and bellowing out edicts concerning what should and shouldn't happen during his next inevitable absence. When he discovered I was ill again, he looked at me in pure disgust.

"What's wrong with you now? Everyone else is fine! I swear, gal, you're more trouble than you're worth!"

"The chile can't help it, Thurston, leave her alone!" Passive except when it came to her children, whom she loved and protected with a fierceness reserved only for them, my mother immediately came to my defense.

But I still thought, *was this why he didn't stay with us?* Was I too much trouble for him? For Momma? For everybody? Terrified that this might be true, I tried first to feign wellness even when I was ill, which was never successful, and secondly, I tried to make myself indispensable to others. From my oldest brother, William, to the baby, Miriam, I saw something in all of them that I felt was missing in me. A talent for taking charge, an interest in music, the ability to draw, dance, or just be the cute baby of the family. All I had to offer, I thought, was service. So I became the good girl; a people pleaser. I learned quickly how to dress and amuse "the baby" to assist my mother. I gave up any semblance of ownership of anything to my siblings. "Yeah, you can have the bigger pencil, the last piece of paper, the best one of the mismatched kitchen chairs to sit in and do your homework. It's okay."

I voluntarily gave up any place or space in that poor close-knit household.

A transformation was initiated for me when I was in third grade. All students were given a mandatory test. The test seemed easy enough, and I took it along with the other students and thought nothing more of it. Sometime later, I heard the teachers talking about the test results in reference to me.

"This is exciting and important! We must talk to her parents," Mrs. McKibben exclaimed. The tone of their conversation quieted when I looked up and they could tell I had become aware of their discussion. Curious, but not really concerned, I decided to wait and talk to my mother about what I had overheard. Their conversation and excitement was quickly explained to me by my obviously proud mother.

"You did very well on your test, baby. You're exceptionally smart, and they want our permission to let you skip a grade. The kids will be a little older than you, but you will be just as smart as they are! We may not have much now, but that won't always be true and I want you to be prepared for everything! What do you think about that?"

"I don't know, Momma. Do you think I can do it?"

"I think all my children can do anything they want to do if they have the chance." All my siblings also encouraged me. Even my oldest brother, then in the Army, wrote a supportive and encouraging letter to me. My brothers and sisters cheered when I told my mother I would try.

That was the start of my metamorphosis. I felt I had gained a place, an identity that I could name. I was smart. And so it was that I skipped third grade and went directly to fourth grade, where I continued to do well. It was in fourth grade that I wrote my earliest poem and won first prize in a contest competing with entrants from schools in various parts of Western Pennsylvania. Fourth graders were also offered a music period, where they could learn a musical instrument, and while I longed to play the violin, I had to settle for the only available instrument, which was the B-flat clarinet. This step resulted in my eventual participation in both the orchestra in junior high and the marching band in high school. I was also encouraged to expand my reading, and through my reading I found the courage to want more. A way out of the impoverished existence that up until now had seemed impossible to escape. It wasn't the magic of a place like Hershey, Pennsylvania with its chocolate promises that initiated the change but the glimpse of a different life—a life filled with possibility and hope just like the implied promise of the lovely globes of Disneyland. I was beginning to know who I could be and where I might be headed. I was Nancy, the smart one. Smart enough to skip a grade, write a poem, learn to play the clarinet, and maybe live a life that, up until now, had existed for me only in books.

Nancy McKeever

A Summons to the Principal's Office

There were three chairs outside the school's main office door. One if you had an appointment with the school nurse, a second if you needed to see the guidance counselor, and a third if you were unfortunate enough to have an appointment with the school principal. This morning the other two chairs were empty, and I occupied the principal's chair. I had been interrupted at the end of Band I class by a senior hall monitor, who walked me to the main office and had me sit in the dreaded chair. "Wait here until someone calls you," he said casually, and slid lazily down the hall.

The chair was a large piece of furniture constructed of dark brown wood. The fabric seat had a worn floral pattern that was slightly scuffed around the edges, evidence of the many students who had sat here anxiously before me. The detail of the wide carved armrests was beginning to be worn smooth by the pressure of countless sweaty little hands. My legs dangled below the seat, and I swung them restlessly as I waited to be called. I peered down the deserted hallway. All the classroom doors were shut, and from behind them I could hear the murmur of classes in session. Mr. Wells teaching math in room 101, Miss Bennett teaching science in room 102, and my favorite teacher, Mrs. Wooley, teaching my favorite subject, English, in room 104. The sun shone brightly through the almost ceiling-high hallway windows, and I could see dust motes floating lazily in the air like snowflakes at the beginning of a snow squall.

Not a soul was in the hallway. I felt marooned on a sea of anxiety. Why was I here? What had I done? Where was Mrs. Beatty, the principal? I thought back over the day thus far. As usual, it had been a good school day. I was a good student who loved school, especially English and reading, and I had the grades to prove it. Homeroom had been just the usual catching up with friends, some exchanging of homework due in another class, and the making of after-school plans. First period science was boring, but Mr. Wells was a would-be comedian and worked hard to make sure everyone enjoyed class while also understanding the work and having a chance to ask questions. Second period was chaotic, because Valerdine Bennet vomited, which was an excuse for everyone to leave their seats and comment on how disgusting it all was. The boys especially had great fun pretending to throw the vomit at the squealing girls in the room. Third period was music with Mr. Costello, and I was just learning how to play the clarinet. My "practice" consisted of my using only the clarinet mouthpiece and reed to make little staccato sounds emerge from the partial instrument.

At home, my older brother accused me of spitting at him, and my entire family was eager for me to pass through this beginner's stage and start to make "real music."

It was at the end of third period that the senior hall monitor had entered the music room and told Mr. Costello that I was to accompany him to the principal's office. So, there I sat, fearfully waiting to be summoned. After what seemed like hours but was perhaps only fifteen minutes, I was called in. Mrs. Beatty rose from her desk to greet me. She was a tall, thin, imposing woman who could make any fourth grader feel very, very small. She wore her hair pulled back in a neat bun and was never seen without her silver glasses, which sometimes hung from a pearl chain around her long, thin neck. After telling me to be seated, she sat down and opened a large brown folder on her desk. She read the contents slowly, then looked up at me and smiled a smile that made her appear younger and much less forbidding.

"Well, Nancy, congratulations on winning the tri-state poetry contest!"

Wow! All of my worrying for nothing! Several months earlier, we had all written poems in English class. I didn't realize these poems would be entered into a contest, and now I had won first prize! My mother, who loved words, reading, and poetry, would be so pleased.

Several weeks after my conversation with Mrs.

Beatty, a special assembly was held announcing the prize, and I was presented with a certificate and a small silver pin with First Place engraved on it. My parents were invited to the ceremony. My father had to work, but my mother, of course, attended. In front of the whole school, I proudly recited my poem, which was titled "Fairies":

> *In the evening at the end of day,*
> *See the fairies dance and play.*
> *Up among the chimney top,*
> *Spinning round and round like tops.*
> *Some sit in the apple trees,*
> *Swaying, swaying with the breeze.*
> *Only the very sharpest eyes,*
> *Can see them dancing through the skies.*
> *But make a little noise and they,*
> *Will open their wings and fly away.*

The class reacted with surprise and delight, clapping their hands with approval. Perhaps this was the start of my new life! Perhaps this is when I first realized the power of writing, and the joyous satisfaction that only writing can bring.

Margaret, Clara, Grandpa, Sarah, and Susie

Nancy and Susie

Susie

Nancy and Susie

SUSIE

The Wordsmith

"If t-o-u-g-h spells *tuff*, and r-o-u-g-h spells *ruff*, why doesn't b-o-u-g-h spell *buff* or c-o-u-g-h spell *cuff*?" That was my mother asking unanswerable questions relating to the English language. She loved to play with words. She also enjoyed reading—fiction, nonfiction, poetry—and completing crossword puzzles. Words, words, words—snatches of phrases from poems, a few lines from a song, or references to famous works of art would pepper her everyday conversations like sprinkles on a cupcake.

How she knew such a variety of things, I'll never know. My mother, Susie Beatrice Burwell, was born on December 24, 1914, in Henderson, North Carolina. One of six children born to a farmer's family, she had a difficult life. She lost her mother when she was just thirteen, and she and her three sisters were raised reluctantly by their mother's older sister, Aunt Sue. The brothers stayed at home on the farm. Although she saw that the girls were clothed and fed with the money sent by their father, Aunt Sue was emotionally harsh and withdrawn.

Having no access to books other than the Bible at home, my mother read voraciously at school. At age fourteen, an eye infection left her almost blind for three months and she remained nearsighted all her life. Aunt Sue's commentary on the situation was that this was proof that my mother "read too much." Married at the young age of eighteen to seventeen-year-old Thurston Flurry, she quickly became a mother. Her marriage was a difficult one, with Thurston being unfaithful from the beginning and babies coming every two years. My mother worked as a domestic, and my father worked in the steel mills, as did many of the unskilled Black and Italian men in Pittsburgh.

As a mother of six in her early thirties, she was a solidly built woman who was five-foot-eight and weighed 180 pounds. She had caramel-colored skin topped by dark brown hair that she wore parted in the middle. As she aged, her hair turned white only on the sides and formed two parentheses that framed her oval-shaped face. Her wide, warm smile showed a small space between her two front teeth, a trait that she passed on to all her children. A broad, welcoming lap and a full, soft bosom rounded out this perfect mother figure.

She encouraged us to read and did not believe in censoring reading material. On Saturdays, pulling a wagon, she would accompany us to the library, urging us to use our library cards to the limit and check out twelve books apiece. Her favorite reading material was poems by Paul Laurence Dunbar, especially one called

"The Party," which she memorized and recited in dialect.

One morning, while watching my sisters and me in various states of undress as we got ready for school, she said "September Morn."

"What's that, Momma?" we asked.

She explained that this was the name of a famous nude painting by a French artist. The next Saturday we examined that painting in a library book, giggling at the nude female figure. Sometimes in the morning she would greet us with "Good morning, glory. Did you see the rain, dear?" (Reindeer.) She would refer to a butterfly as a "flutter-by." Or, if we mispronounced a word, she'd say, "You put the accent on the wrong syl-lab-le." Silly, trivial sayings, but ones that stay with me after all these years.

Here's another example of a typical "Susieism," as we sometimes called her sayings. I had just graduated from nursing school and was starting my first job. As a new graduate, I was assigned the unpopular night shift and worked 11 p.m. to 7:30 a.m. Each night as I prepared to leave the house and walk the three blocks to catch the trolley, my mother would recite a few lines from the old song "I'll Be Seeing You." The lines she quoted were *I'll see you in the morning sun and when the night is through*. And my response was to be *I'll be looking at the moon, but I'll be seeing you*. I worked nights for seven months before being transferred to the 3 p.m. to 11:30

p.m. shift. Each night for seven months my loving mother sent me off to work using an old song to say "I love you, and I'll see you in the morning."

My children also benefited from my mother's quick wit and love of words. When I worked the 3 p.m. to 11:30 p.m. shift, my mother was also my babysitter. What a treat to come home to find the children bathed and in bed, the house neat, and my dinner waiting for me! The next day they would tell me about Grandma reading stories or hiding behind the sofa when they played hide-and-seek. My daughter, soon to be forty-five, remembers how my mother explained some concept to her, and when my daughter said, "I see," my mother said in response, "I see said the blind man to his deaf daughter as he picked up his hammer and saw." Silly and nonsensical, but that has stuck with my daughter all these years.

As my mother grew older, she became shorter in stature and her shoulders rounded with age; however, her mind remained sharp and inquisitive. At the age of ninety-three years, she decided to write a poem. It was titled "A Father's Night Before Christmas." In it, she told the story of a ten-year-old boy who pretended to be drunk on Christmas Eve. She wrote the poem, had my sister print it out, and mailed a copy to each one of her children. She was highly offended at our surprise that she had taken on this task at her age.

She faced many hardships in her life—racism, poverty, too many children, an unfaithful husband, the loss of both an infant son from pneumonia at age eleven months, and in later years a forty-nine-year-old son to complications of AIDS. Despite a mastectomy in her seventies, a colostomy in her eighties, and finally a brain tumor in her nineties, my mother somehow found the strength to be loving, vibrant, playful, and present for her children and grandchildren. Living fully, savoring every pleasurable event that came her way, and sharing her joy with her family, she persevered. She had her faults, as all humans do, but by any standards she was a truly remarkable woman.

Nancy McKeever

Overpaid

My mother told me this story, and this is how I imagined it happened. She was on her way to the trolley stop after cleaning Mrs. Howarth's house. She made her way down the hot pavement, waves of heat bouncing off the asphalt like a rubber ball. Wednesday was one of her easier house-cleaning days. The house was never really dirty, mostly dusty from the hot August wind blowing the humid air around. The biggest task was changing the bed, but even then, she enjoyed the sharp crack of the sheets as she shook them loose from their folds. She took pleasure in smoothing out all the wrinkles, tucking the hospital corners, and plumping up the huge pillows. When finished, the bed always reminded her of something out of *House Beautiful*.

Mrs. Howarth was seemingly a kind woman. Short in stature, she was of slight build and had dark, gray-streaked hair and bright eyes. In repose, one side of her face drooped slightly, the residual of a bout of Ménière's disease, which had occurred a few months earlier. She looked like a small inquisitive bird as she moved around the kitchen making lunch for both of them; something simple but delicious. That day it had been egg salad on wheat bread with thinly sliced tomatoes. A tall, frosty glass of iced tea stood next to each plate, and beside that on a small saucer was one oatmeal raisin cookie. Many times, my mother wondered if this sharing of a meal was more for Mrs. Howarth than for her, as she seemed to enjoy the company and a chance for a friendly chat.

Mrs. Howarth had one son, an attorney in New York, and a daughter, an artist who lived in San Francisco. Even though they both visited every few months, she missed them terribly and would often remark to my mother, "Enjoy them while you can." Each discussed their offspring proudly.

As she made her way down the hot pavement, my mother dug into her scuffed purse with its slightly worn lining to pull out the money Mrs. Howarth had handed to her as she left for the day. She unfolded the bills and began counting: One-two-three-four-five-six! She stopped walking and re-counted the bills in her hand. One-two-three-four-five-six! She was paid five dollars a day and been overpaid by one dollar. Should she keep the money? Was it a mistake? Was it a test? Mrs. Howarth seemed friendly enough, but you never knew. Maybe she could just keep the money and explain to Mrs. Howarth when she returned next week. She could take four dollars on that day rather than her usual five. If she kept it, she could buy a small piece of ham to go in the lima beans for tonight's dinner. Lima beans were not her children's favorite, but the ham would be a treat.

She still could not decide what to do. She was only one block from the bus stop, and returning the money would mean making the trip back to Mrs. Howarth's house and retracing her steps in the relentless sun. She would miss her usual trolley home and would arrive there a half hour later. The children, always so eager to see her, would be waiting on the corner outside the tenement building where they lived. Pressing their ears against the telephone pole, they would listen for the hum of the trolley. They could hear it long before it rounded the bend on Oakwood Street and rocked slowly on the rails toward home.

Oh well, she couldn't go on. She had to take the extra money back. She turned and trudged back down the street. She rang the bell. As she waited, she realized she was holding her breath. Mrs. Howarth answered the door and chirped in a surprised voice, "Susie, what's wrong?"

"You overpaid me. You gave me a dollar extra," my mother said, holding out the unfolded bills.

"Oh, Susie," Mrs. Howarth exclaimed. "It was my mistake. Keep the dollar and I'll see you next week!"

My mother thanked her, turned, and once again made her way to the trolley stop. As she retraced her steps, she let out a sigh of relief and chuckled quietly to herself. How silly of her to get so worked up over such a minor incident. It was just a human mistake. An extra dollar. Now she could stop at the butcher's on Homewood Avenue and get a small piece of ham with the bone in. She rode the gently swaying trolley as it wound its way toward home. She thought of her children's happy faces and smiled.

Homewood Avenue was the main thoroughfare of this poor Black and Italian section of Pittsburgh. Four long blocks that snaked downhill. It held a grocery store, a butcher shop, a five-and-ten, a bakery, a movie theater, a shoemaker, a cleaner, and other smaller businesses. On Saturdays it was busy and bustling, but today it would be less crowded. Fifteen minutes after that, she would reach the alley that led into Oakwood Street and home. She'd walk quickly so her children would not have too long to wait.

The trolley rolled up the street as she neared the corner. Good, no waiting. She boarded and settled into her seat with a tired but contented sigh.

Imagine the children's faces when she emerged from the alley. They knew if she came that way, she had stopped on Homewood Avenue and had some special treat. She could hear them now, "Mommy, did you bring us a surprise?"

She in turn could honestly answer in the affirmative

and tell them she had enough for a double treat. It was turning out to be a great day!

Purple Memory

1.

This is how I first imagined the story. My mother, seven months pregnant, went to the Wilkinsburg Hospital Emergency Room. She had gone to the ladies' room to replace the now soggy newspaper lining her shoes with dry paper towels while waiting for the staff to call her. The waiting made her angry, but she couldn't afford to cause a scene. Her baby was sick and needed attention. The staff in the emergency room had been cold but efficient. She had had to wait, of course, and watch the age-old practice of treating white people, whether adults or children, first. They kept saying, "Just a few more minutes and we will be with you." It was all part of being Black and poor in Pittsburgh, Pennsylvania, in the 1940s. Everything was a struggle; life one long uphill battle. But who could refuse to treat a sick baby no matter the color of his/her skin? After what seemed to be a very cursory examination, the doctor diagnosed baby Curt as "congested" and ordered an aspirin suppository to be given immediately and cough medicine to be given at home. She begged the doctor to admit her son, but he said it wasn't necessary. Curt was only eleven months old, still so very little, and had been sick for three days. My mother had been reluctant to take him out into the snow, but his fever just would not go down and he remained fussy and sleepless. He seemed quiet now. Maybe the suppository had helped him sleep.

At least she would start her return trip with her feet a little bit drier. She walked back home through the deserted, quiet and snowy streets. She felt so alone, as if she were the only person awake in the world. All the homes on the street were dark, with not one sliver of light shining through any window. Every door and window was tightly locked against the harsh Pittsburgh winter. She was the only thing moving on the street. Even the trolleys had not started their initial run of the day as it was not yet 5 a.m. She was now on Oakwood Street, the street on which she lived, but she still had ten blocks to go.

The melting snow felt like a small, cold worm as it made its way through the paper towels that she had stuffed in her worn-out shoes. She knew that the paper wouldn't hold but had hoped to be closer to home before it actually soaked through. She couldn't dwell on it now and needed to concentrate on getting home and putting her sick baby boy to bed after giving him a dose of the medication received from the hospital.

As she slowly made her way toward home, she passed what was called the "Old Folks Home," a nursing facility for senior citizens. The curved porch, which ran the length of the building, was bare now except for drifts of snow that had blown against its red brick walls. In the summertime you'd see the seniors lined up on this same porch, their row of black rocking chairs looking very much like crows perched on a curved telephone line. Now she was nearing Elizabeth and Walter's house. Elizabeth was Thurston's older sister and was newly married at age fifty-two to construction worker Walter. She was bubbly and vivacious, and he was big, burly, and intimidating, but they seemed good together. Their sturdy three-story brick house was home to Elizabeth, Walter, and one tenant. How Susie would have loved to live in a house that size with her children. Enough living space and bedrooms for everyone. The thought of it made her smile as she continued her cold, wet journey home.

Five houses farther down the street from Elizabeth lived Susie's sister, Clara; her favorite sister who was two years older than she. Clara would be up now, having a leisurely cup of coffee as this was her off day from her six-day-a-week job as a domestic. It would be nice to stop in and have a cup of coffee and maybe even change the paper towels in her shoes. But no, she needed to get home, get Curt settled, and wake her other children for school.

She was so tired. Maybe after the other children were in school, she could find something for her three-year-old to do while she took a short nap with the baby.

Her husband was not at home, again. He was staying with that woman in East Liberty as he did for weeks at a time. Someday she would give him an ultimatum about his comings and goings, but she was too exhausted to think about that now.

Finally, she could see the two-story tenement building where they lived. She, Thurston, and six children in two rooms. They shared an adjoining bathroom with her sister Sarah and Sarah's husband, Tom. An arrangement which was at times unsatisfactory for all. When she would get angry about some imagined slight, Sarah would rant about "all those damn Flurrys," but most of the time things were congenial between the two families.

At last, she was home. She slowly climbed the stairs to the second floor. The building smelled of oil because the landlord, Mr. Vaughn, would coat the wooden hallways with oil to "keep the dust down." This was a problem in the summertime as her girls would sit in the hallway to play and get oil on their summer dresses and white socks. It took a lot of scrubbing on the washboard to get rid of those stubborn oil spots.

My mother quietly let herself into the apartment. Everyone was still asleep. She placed the still-sleeping infant near the middle of her double bed. Waking him briefly to medicate him, she then tucked him in snugly. Now to get off her wet shoes. Soggy paper towel clung to her wet socks, and she rubbed her toes until she could begin to feel them again. Stuffing her wet shoes with newspaper, she sat them beside the little open flame stove that she lit in the bedroom. This would warm up the room for her other children, who would soon be up getting ready for school. She eased quietly down onto her bed and could still hear the cold rattling in Curt's little chest. She lay down beside him to rest for just a minute. So very tired. She awoke with a start. How long had she been asleep? What time was it? She looked at the small clock that sat on the tiny three-legged table beside the bed. Six-thirty—half an hour before she had to wake the other children. Time to check Curt's temperature. He was quiet, and she could no longer hear his labored breathing. Had one suppository and one dose of medication worked so quickly? She went to the mantel to get the thermometer she'd placed there earlier. Pulling back the blanket, she went to take the baby's temperature. He was cold. And still. Not breathing. Oh God, no, he couldn't be dead. Did he choke while she was sleeping, and she didn't hear him? Why did she allow herself to fall asleep? She felt as if all her blood was leaving her body, as if she might faint. She collapsed on the bed beside the small, still body. In death, he looked like a sleeping baby doll with one small hand tucked under his left cheek. Tears of rage ran down her face. Tears for the circumstances that caused her to have to carry him through the snow; tears for him being denied admission; and tears that her husband was not there to comfort her over the death of their son.

She looked down at the small body lying so still beneath the blankets. She had now lost one child while carrying yet another. What other depths of despair would she be forced to experience in this lifetime? No time to question. No time to grieve. No time to rest. She allowed herself one last release of tears, then dried her eyes and rose to wake her other children.

2.

This is the story I had written some years ago when I was attempting to write about my younger brother's death. I wrote it as I remembered it; after all, I was very young then, not quite five years old. It wasn't until I was cleaning out my mother's house after her death that I questioned my memory.

I was seeing at least one item for the second time. On my yearly visits, my mother often asked me to retrieve one box from the neatly stacked pile in her basement. In this particular box, lying haphazardly among many other papers was a small, cheaply made book. It appeared to be approximately eight inches by five inches, with covers made of cardboard. The cardboard was covered in a thin sheet of dark purple paper and very worn, as if it had been handled many times. The front cover was almost completely separated from the back. When opened, the following statistics were filled out in my mother's meticulous handwriting: Name: Curtland Douglas Flurry. DOB: 06/20/1946. DOD: 5/27/1947. I read on but was drawn back to that first page by the date of death, 5/27/1947. Why had I thought Curt had died in the winter? Why did I think this and why had I not recognized the importance of the dates, an importance that still eluded me. I remained confused for a moment, and it took a few seconds to calm my thoughts and my breathing as I began to cull additional information from our family history. I was born May 29, 1942. Curt was born in June 1946, and Mimsi was born July 26, 1947. I tried to think calmly. What was I trying to get to? Maybe I needed to start over. Curt was born in 1946 and died in 1947. Mimsi, five years younger than me, was born in July 1947. That means that my mother was already seven months pregnant with Mimsi when Curt died. I also finally understood the other significance (at least to me) of the date of death. May 27—my brother had died just two days before my fifth birthday.

Did I have a cake that year? Did everyone just forget my birthday and go on as if it were just an ordinary day, although the day must have been anything but ordinary? Did my mother not make one of her magnificent cakes?

I remember very little about that day or any of the days that followed. I do remember Curt, bundled in white, lying in a small white box in Aunt Sarah's living room. He looked like he was sleeping. I don't remember my kindergarten class coming to our home. But this fact is substantiated by the little purple book, which has space for attendees to sign their names. There is indeed a list of names. Why would anyone have allowed a kindergarten class to visit under these circumstances? My mother would have been only thirty-three years old. I can't imagine what she was feeling. Five children and a sixth on the way. One child who was now deceased.

Once I discovered this, I spent a lot of time talking to Mimsi, my closest sister, and to my therapist, examining my memories and trying to understand this very significant time in my life. Had I misremembered Curt's death happening in the winter to separate those two days?

I still don't understand all of it, but it taught me that memories can indeed be an accurate picture of a certain period in your life, and you carry them because of their significance to you, but sometimes they can be far from the truth, and you remember things in the way that gives you the most comfort. But if you're lucky, comforting or not, somehow the truth will find you.

Judy

Chuckie

Billy

Mimsi

Snip

Nancy

FAMILY LIFE

The Candy Man

"Who's that man who brings the candy?" said my five-year-old sister Mimsi as she sat on the kitchen floor slowly savoring the last bites of a milk chocolate Hershey bar.

Eight-year-old Judy, who was already known for her direct approach to any subject, said, "Dummy, that's our father! He just doesn't live here all the time."

That seemed to satisfy Mimsi. Maybe even at this young age, she had already learned that in this household, there were some things that you didn't question but just accepted as fact. Being the oldest of the three of us, at age ten, I did not even attempt to explain to them things that I myself did not yet understand.

All I knew for sure was that this was Daddy, a man who came and went at intervals and was sometimes gone for weeks. His reappearance was usually timed for the afternoon, when we were in school and Mimsi was home from her morning session of kindergarten. Bringing a Hershey bar for Mimsi and chocolate-covered cherries for my mother, he would act as if he had been away only a few hours rather than a few weeks.

"Nancy, Judy, Mimsi! It's eight o'clock and time to get up! If I'm up, everybody's up!"

That was my father as he stood at the bottom of the stairs and bellowed up to the second floor. A short, stocky man with a deep bass voice, his directive reverberated throughout the small two-bedroom, one-bath house where we lived in Pittsburgh, Pennsylvania. He was short in stature, but his presence was huge. He woke us up just because he could. That was his M.O., his way of reinforcing the fact that he was the boss, the king of the household.

In response to his command to get up, we answered immediately, saying "Yes, Daddy" in unison while grumbling softly to each other. The three of us shared one of the bedrooms in the house. Mimsi, my younger sister, and my responsibility from birth, slept with me. Judy slept alone as my mother deemed her "too sensitive and finicky" to sleep with anyone else.

"Why does he wake us up at eight o'clock on Saturday? We did all our work yesterday, even the laundry," Judy whispered angrily.

"Why does she let him do that?" I said. "Why doesn't she stick up for us?"

From Mimsi, "I bet now he goes out, just like always."

Sure enough, as we reluctantly got out of bed and moved sluggishly around the room, we heard the front door open and then close. Looking out the bedroom window, we saw our father cross the street in front of our house, cut through Dave's gas station and head down Bennett Street toward East Liberty. He walked steadily, his short legs pumping, his almost bald head with his ever-present "newsboy cap" slightly lowered. He made me think of a bulldog, tenacious in appearance and actions.

A few minutes later, we heard the stairs creak as my mother came upstairs. We immediately started in.

"Why does he do that? Why do we have to get up? Why can't we ever just sleep late?"

My mother replied with her usual response: "You know how your father is."

I heard that phrase many times during my childhood.

My father was the undisputed boss of the house and never let anyone forget it. He dictated the rules, and everyone followed them, resentfully but without question. He was especially hard on the girls and belittled us in words and actions, making us clean up after our brothers and constantly reminding us of "our place" in life. In his mind, women only needed to be good wives and mothers and had no need to aim for anything more. He made it clear that once we graduated from high school, we would be expected to work for at least a year to "put money back into the house" before we married.

My mother spoke up for the first time I can remember when I won a scholarship to nursing school. Of course, my father did not want me to go.

"She could be working," he stormed at my mother.

She said firmly, "Thurston, they will pay for everything. It won't cost us a penny!"

"She won't get a penny from me," he said angrily. True to his word, he never gave me one cent during the years I was in school. My mother and oldest brother and older sister saw that I had a little spending money each week. Years later, my father would smile and call me his "Nancy Nurse." He had nothing to do with it. Had he forgotten?

He neither smoked nor drank, loved to play bridge, and listened to spirituals on Sunday mornings. He spent his life working as a stoker in the steel mill, a job that required him to shovel coal directly into the huge furnace used to melt the steel. When dressing for work, he had to wear two sets of long underwear, two shirts, and thick pants to protect himself from an errant ember. Even with all this, he still had burns on his arms and his back, and his work clothes were dotted with burn holes. I remember once riding with my older brother Billy when we took our father to work for the three to eleven shift. I watched him as he walked down a long ramp leading to what appeared to be an endless dark hole ending directly below the furnaces. As he slowly melted into the blackness, I thought to myself, *No wonder he's so mean. How can he do this every day?*

As I grew older and overheard conversations between my mother and her sisters and questioned my older brothers and sister, I found out the reason for my father's absences. It turns out he had another family. While we were living in indescribable poverty, he was spending time and what little money he earned with another woman and their children. Was he nicer to them? Did they get more of his money? When the steelworkers went on strike did they have to stand in the free food line accepting the handouts given to the strikers' families? My mother knew about the other woman and children but still allowed him to move back and forth between the two families. At one point, the other woman (I never knew her name) had the gall to call our house and ask to speak to our mother. I happened to answer the phone. It was a surreal experience. I could hear my father's distinctive deep voice in the background as he demanded that she hang up the phone. After the whispers about her all these years, there she was on the other end of the phone! I alerted my sister Judy to pick up the upstairs extension and between the two of us we called this woman every derogatory name we could think of. She in turn called for my father to come to the phone saying, "You say they're so smart, but you should hear what language they're using now!" My father never came to the phone, and we hung up once we ran out of adjectives. The specifics of that conversation with her faded after a while, but I never forgot that she said that he'd called us "smart." It was only after my father returned home for good that I found out that my mother had accepted him back permanently only after he signed over his retirement benefits and life insurance to her and promised never to see this woman again. When my mother died at age ninety-four, she was still receiving benefits from the United Steelworkers union.

Although none of us girls forgot the fact that for a long time my father's life was divided between two families, somehow it became less of a conscious issue once he definitely settled in with our mother and we had families of our own.

It wasn't until my father's death that any thoughts of residual resentment pushed themselves to any conscious level. As we prepared to fly to Pittsburgh for his funeral, Mimsi and I had repeated conversations about the fact that neither of us felt badly enough about his death to cry.

"How can you not cry at your father's funeral?" I said. "People will think it's strange and Momma will be so upset, but I don't feel like crying. I worry about Momma being alone but crying for Thurston (for now he was Thurston, not Daddy). No, I'm not there."

All four of us discussed this and the sentiment was the same. Finally, Judy, Miss No-Nonsense, said, "Look, we just have to fake it! We'll use a handkerchief or a bunch of Kleenex, anything to cover our bone-dry faces. If one of those church people from Saint Mark's approaches us, we'll just be too upset to talk. It's settled!" And that was the plan.

On the day of the funeral, family and friends gathered in the chapel in the mortuary. "Amazing Grace" played softly as members of the immediate family were escorted in one by one. My mother was first, holding tightly to my oldest brother's arm as she wept softly. My older sister Snip was next escorted by my cousin Richie, and I was behind her accompanied by my cousin Bobby. I felt sad but also strangely detached from the proceedings. I wondered how my sisters felt but there was no way to tell. Judy's son walked with her, and Mimsi was last with her husband, Robert.

My mother reached the casket first and stood for a few minutes looking down at her husband. She began to cry even harder. My brother put his arm around her shoulders and led her to her seat. As my sisters and I reached my father, each of our escorts stepped back so just the four of us surrounded the casket.

I looked down at my father who seemed to be resting peacefully. He looked younger to me, but he also looked very small. It was hard to believe that this was the same man who had bullied us throughout our childhood.

Although no one said a word, my sisters and I spontaneously linked arms like a human chain, looked down at "Daddy" and cried.

Crowning Glory

A woman's hair used to be referred to as her "crowning glory." For a Black woman, this was far from true. Hair maintenance was a major undertaking. This was especially true in our household, where there were four daughters.

In Pittsburgh in the 1940s, there was no Black Power and Black certainly was not considered beautiful. The goal, as far as hair was concerned, was to be as white as possible. This meant, for a young Black female, that each time her hair was shampooed, it had to be followed by a torturous process known as "straightening." Shampoo day in our house was a long, arduous procedure involving four girls who argued about who went first the last time, who would be first today, and who could manipulate to go last in hopes that Momma would be too tired to complete head number four. My mother led the players in this shampoo drama. She was a tall, statuesque woman, solidly built, but not at all fat. She had an ample lap on which to cuddle more than one small child at a time, and being full-breasted, she could easily nestle a head while soothing hurts physical or emotional. With her engaging and fun-loving personality, she would easily pull pranks on you, throw out random quotes from literature, make a play on words, or neatly complete the Sunday crossword puzzle in ink.

Of my sisters, Shirley, the eldest, better known as Snip, was older than me by seven years. I thought she was beautiful, sophisticated, and knowledgeable of all things worldly. She was also bored to tears by her younger siblings and lamented loudly about her responsibilities as the oldest girl. Two years my junior was Judy. Cute, petite, and fastidious, she reminded me of a whippet, always moving and full of nervous energy. She loved to dance and was always the first to learn and master any new step. Last but not least was Miriam, fondly known as Mimsi. Five years younger than me, she was everyone's darling and was spoiled as only a youngest child can be.

The day started early, with my mother first washing and then braiding everyone's hair. We had no shower, so the shampoos took place in the kitchen sink. The sink counter in this cold-water tenement building was made of wood slats that, due to the washing of dishes and daily use, would stay wet for days at a time. Occasionally in the summertime, the old wooden sink would become infested with maggots. My mother drenched them in boiling water to get rid of them. On shampoo day, my mother heated up several large pots of water. We would lie face up on the damp sink while she washed our hair and rinsed it by maneuvering our head to the correct angle under the faucet.

I always imagined maggots on the sink. My mother would patiently explain that there were no maggots and if I would just lie still, she would be finished shortly.

I was the second oldest girl, but the middle child. Quiet, shy and studious, I was known as "the bookworm." My father used to say that I even enjoyed reading cereal boxes.

After the shampoo, my mother dried and detangled our hair. She then sectioned it off, applied Royal Crown hair pomade, and braided it, eight braids on each side. Once your hair was washed and braided you got a break, and three of us would play jacks or War while my mother shampooed the remaining sister's hair. I really wanted to read but would be pressed into playing games to keep the already tenuous peace.

Next came the straightening part of the procedure. When it was my turn, my mother sat in a kitchen chair at the stove with me sitting on a stool between her legs. My back would be facing her to give her access to all parts of my head and to other parts of my body, for I would sometimes squirm and be rewarded with a firm rap on the shoulder for not sitting still. The straightening comb or straightening iron was a metal comb with a wooden handle. The teeth were curved and darkened with age while the handle was nicked in several places, the paint worn off from many firm grips. It had a scattering of burn spots from being placed too close to an open flame.

The comb was heated over the flame until it was hot enough to be moved through the hair to straighten it but not so hot that it would burn the hair off. This was a delicate balance to achieve, and my mother made repeated temperature testings with moistened fingers as progress was made. These steps were taken with each braid as my mother slowly made her way around my head. The cramped kitchen became warmer as she worked, and the air felt heavy as a woolen blanket, thick with the smell of singed hair. As I sat there, I could hear the bounce of the rubber ball and the skittering of the jacks as they danced across the cracked but clean linoleum floor as my sisters played jacks, or the slap of cards if the game was War. When completed, my hair would be straight and shiny, floating lightly around my head. The final step was to braid our hair neatly into two braids with a brightly colored ribbon attached to each end. When she was at last finished, I would admire my hair from all possible angles in our old tarnished mirror. At that moment, the torture would all seem worthwhile.

When my mother was especially energetic, she would give us all bangs. This was accomplished by using yet another tool called a curling iron. It very much resembled the curling irons of today, except the irons were smaller in circumference. This again required the heat of an open flame and repeated temperature testing. My mother would part off an appropriate amount of hair and then curl it tightly because the curls easily loosened as we played. It didn't help that we deliberately shook our heads just to feel the whisper of the bangs on our foreheads.

I look at my old school pictures and in each one, my hair is freshly "done" with bangs, and I think back to those days of sitting between my mother's legs as she made sure that I looked "presentable." It was only after I was grown with daughters of my own that I began to question the hair straightening ritual. What did it mean that I put my daughters and myself through such a harrowing process to change a basic trait about us? What did it mean for my self-esteem growing up in a society where the Breck girl was the epitome of beauty and looked nothing like me? Was I ashamed to be Black? Did I not think a natural hairstyle was beautiful? It was years before I could answer these questions.

One Sunday afternoon while I was visiting my mother, my sister Judy, her husband George (a professor of Black Studies at Duquesne University), and my five-year-old nephew Ebon also stopped by. We were very surprised to see them all sporting full Afros. My mother was horrified as only a woman of her generation could be, but I thought, how freeing!

Knowing my mother would disapprove, I said nothing at first but was soon also proudly wearing an Afro. Self-conscious at first, I repeatedly touched my hair or checked it out in the bathroom mirror to make sure it was still properly in place. Did I feel more Black with an Afro? No, but I felt proud and comfortable. After about a year, I went back to straightened hair. I made the decision with no guilt or judgment.

As the years have passed, my daughters and I have gone through various hairstyles: perms, weaves, extensions, and chemical straighteners. At this point in our lives, none of us requires the use of a straightening comb but it still lives, scarred, nicked, and scorched on the top shelf of my eldest daughter's linen closet. She calls it our family "hairloom."

A Family Affair

I always felt as if she tried to wake us more gently on Saturdays. Certainly, she was well aware of the difficult task that lay before us and maybe in her own way was trying to say "I'm sorry." She started prepping her famous cinnamon rolls on Friday (if all the ingredients were available) in anticipation of the troublesome Saturdays; but we knew our real reward for getting through Saturday with as little complaint and squabble as possible would be to awaken Sunday morning to the mouthwatering smell of the rolls. The crowded apartment rooms would be filled with the scrumptious aroma of butter, cinnamon, vanilla, and all the other ingredients that when mixed together resulted in her delicious rolls. So we dragged ourselves reluctantly out of bed with the wonderful memories of yesterday's biscuits still in our minds and the promise of additional goodies yet to come.

It was on Saturday that we did the weekly spraying for bedbugs. Roaches got hit also if they happened to be lurking in the same area, but bedbugs were really our target. Sometimes in the winter, we would skip a Saturday. They didn't seem to like the colder weather, but we never skipped in the summer when the heat was a catalyst, encouraging the bugs to multiply. Getting dressed and having breakfast was a quick affair, especially if there were biscuits left over from the day before. While we ate, my mother gathered the necessary equipment. First, bug spray—I have no knowledge of its true name—to us it was just "the spray." (I wonder now if it was DDT, later banned for causing cancer.) She then gathered the sprayers. Each one was a strange-looking contraption with a long arm that was attached to a circular container with an opening in the top allowing one to pour the spray into it. On the opposite end of the arm was a plunger that allowed you to forcibly push the liquid out in a strong spray. Each of us was assigned a corner of the bed, and one person was assigned "broom duty" to sweep up the bug remains.

First, the sheets were removed from the beds. You'd always see a few bedbugs running about trying to avoid the light. Sometimes they would quickly scramble back into one of the many cracks in the old plaster walls, but we knew we'd eventually spray the cracks also. The next step was to actually remove the mattress from the metal springs. What looked like thousands of bedbugs would be teeming over the bedsprings, running and tumbling over each other. At times the bed seemed alive and actually moving.

Most of the bugs seemed to head for the corners of the bedsprings, and since there was not enough room for all of them, they would just fall helplessly to the floor to then be sprayed again, die, and then be swept up by the person who was handling broom duty that day. This procedure was performed on two beds, the crib, and the rollaway bed, which was stored in the kitchen. By the time we were finished, the floors were wet with spray and brown with the bodies of so many bedbugs. The apartment, even with both of its small windows open, was cloudy with the fog of spray, and its pungent smell. We would repeat this procedure until there was absolutely no sighting of the pests, but there always seemed to be at least one of them still crawling. Once, my brother continued to spray almost in a frenzy until my mother, touching him gently on his arm, said firmly "Stop, you've used more than enough spray on this one bug." Cleanup was done quickly and efficiently with all traces of our work disposed of. Spray put away, floor swept and scrubbed, beds wiped down and then made with clean sheets. But the smell was hard to erase. Even after the fog dissipated, the odor lingered in the air for hours as if to remind us that we could not eradicate all traces of the bugs no matter how hard we tried.

Once this chore was completed, we could relax for the rest of the day. I would read; the others played cards or read comic books. We would try to think of my mother's promised cinnamon rolls rather than think of the next wave of bedbugs that we knew, despite all of our work that day, would reappear again that night.

My Billy

Flurry, William Henry Flurry. Long before the days of James Bond, this is the way my oldest brother introduced himself. We knew him as Billy. He was ten years my senior, and I always saw him as strong, handsome, confident, and sophisticated. He had a wide, warm smile and, when talking with him, you felt as if you were the most important person in the world. Taller than my father, he stood five feet eleven inches tall. He had dark brown skin and short cropped hair. In an old black-and white-family photo, my brother sits erect staring straight into the camera. He's positioned to the left of my mother, his right shoulder slightly in front of her as if protecting her from the world. This is a position he took literally and figuratively as he fell into the role of father figure early in his life. My father was not always faithful to my mother and spent long periods of time away from home. This left my brother, the oldest of seven children, in the position of being the man of the house long before he was a man.

When we were older and discussed our early childhood, he told me, "I felt like I had six children."

I can see why he felt this way. Time and time again, he instinctively stepped into the role of father or leader of us all.

Nancy McKeever

I remember his actions one rainy Saturday afternoon. At that time, Billy was eighteen years old; Snip was fifteen; Charles (Chuckie) was twelve; I was ten; Judith (Judy) was eight; and Miriam (Mimsi) was five. My mother was washing clothes in our small kitchen. Wash day for my mother meant washing clothes by hand using a washtub, a washboard on which to rub the clothes, and a bar of Octagon or Fels-Naptha laundry soap. Usually the clothes were washed and then dried by hanging them on a clothesline outside. On a rainy day, such as this, the clothes were dried inside, hung from a clothesline that crisscrossed the kitchen. This meant ducking under towels, undershirts, and other clothing as we made our way around the kitchen. No one was in the best of spirits that day. Rain meant we could not play outside and had to put up with each other inside the house. Six children, one adult, and two rooms. Not enough space to go around. There were many attempts at playing the few games available to us, but each game ended in a heated argument about someone playing out of turn, touching someone's cards, or adding up the score incorrectly. The final straw for my mother was an argument between Chuckie and Judy. We were playing cards with a deck pieced together from multiple old decks. Everyone always knew who had the ace of spades and the two of hearts because their backs were red and the rest of the deck was blue. Judy accused Chuckie of dealing himself the two red-backed cards so he would be sure of getting an ace. The squabble resulted first in an exchange of words and dissolved into a shoving match that ended with Judy bursting into tears. My mother had had enough.

She said sternly, "That's it! Each of you sit down, do not talk, and do not move until I finish these clothes!"

Well, that was it. Not only could we not go outside, we had to sit silently in the tiny kitchen amid all those wet clothes and do nothing but glower at each other. After what seemed like an eternity, there was a knock at the door.

"Get the door, Chuckie," my mother said. The door was opened and in walked Billy. He didn't live with us as there was not enough room in our small apartment. He rented a room in the home of one of my father's friends.

"Hey everyone," he said.

Noticing the obvious tension in the room, he looked at my mother.

"I'm ready to throw them all out into the rain; I've had enough," she said.

With what seemed like only a moment's hesitation, Billy took off his jacket and reached to turn up the volume on the little radio that sat atop the old icebox beside the door.

"Follow me," he said to us while winking at my mother.

Nancy McKeever

The radio blasted "Shake, Rattle and Roll" by Bill Haley and His Comets. Before my mother could say anything, we were up from our seats and forming a line behind my brother. Billy snatched up the nearest towel from off the line. Placing one end of the towel in his mouth, he used his hands to shape the towel into a crude saxophone. With the towel in place, he began prancing through the house with us following behind him. Snip twirled her skirt like a can-can girl; Chuckie drummed on chairs, tables, and anything else within reach. I followed close behind Chuckie and clapped gleefully. Judy, the dancer of the group, floated behind me trying out new steps all the way. Last was baby sister Mimsi, who skipped to keep up with the rest of us.

Around the kitchen we snaked, below the wet clothes and around the table, past the rollaway bed sitting in the corner, where Chuckie and Judy slept head to foot each night, past the cabinets full of clean but mismatched dishes. A left turn took us into the bedroom. It was a tight squeeze to make it in between the double bed where my mother, and sometimes my father, slept. We made our way behind Mimsi's crib and then passed in front of the big old Philco radio with one missing dial so you could never get treble but always had plenty of bass. One last curve took us past the single bed that Snip and I shared and where, unbelievably, my cousin Tiki also slept when she chose to spend the night. Continuing on, we passed the little open-flame stove that helped heat the room in the winter, and finally headed back into the kitchen, where my mother sat smiling. One last turn around her chair and the song ended. We collapsed, laughing, into our chairs while my mother clapped enthusiastically, and Billy took a bow.

The whole atmosphere in the apartment had changed. Thanks to Billy, it didn't matter that it was raining, and that the kitchen was small, damp, and crowded. It didn't matter that we played with mismatched cards and had cramped sleeping quarters. In those few joyful moments, we had gone from six disgruntled children dissatisfied with the world and with each other to a fun-loving family. We were reminded of the true love we had for each other, and that was definitely enough.

Nancy McKeever

Dancing Queen

You are the dancing queen
Young and sweet
Only seventeen
Dancing queen.

This 1970s song by ABBA could have been written about my sister Judy, as, in my mind, she was the "Dancing Queen" of our family. A small wisp of a girl, she was certainly a standout on the dance floor. Petite, with cocoa-colored skin and trend-setting styled hair, she floated to the music in an effortless way. No matter the song, old or new, she absorbed the beat and made it her own. She was always first to incorporate a new dance into her repertoire and even made up her own steps at times. I sometimes thought that Judy chose her many boyfriends and even her husband by the way they danced.

She married a man who, though he appeared overweight, was extremely light on his feet and matched her dance skills perfectly. Seeing them together on the dance floor was always a treat. Many times, when they got up to perform, everyone else would clear the floor and then give them a round of applause when they finished. I used to wish feverishly that I had even a little of my sister's dancing talent so that I could 'keep up' with my older brother Chuckie. My father would only allow me to go to parties to which my brother was also invited. Chuckie, while not as talented as Judy, loved to dance and certainly surpassed me in his dancing skills. He used to beg me to "practice" routines before parties so that we'd be sure to look good. His reasoning was that I would be less anxious and so would perform better. Wrong. No amount of practicing decreased my anxiety. Judy seemed to understand my feelings, although she, too, seemed to believe that I could do better with a little more practice.

The junior/senior dance was approaching, and I really wanted to go. The dance was only held once a year, and while I usually was not especially interested in attending, this year I knew that Clyde Phelps would be attending. Clyde, a member of the senior class, was my idea of the perfect date. Yes, he was short, as my sister reminded me, but he was also smart and kind, a bookworm type, and the only person who noticed when I made my first stab at trying eyebrow pencil. Even Joanne, my best friend, did not immediately notice it. But Clyde, from the other side of the classroom, had pointed at his eyebrows and nodded yes. Surely that had meant he approved. Or did it? Yes, I'm sure that's what it meant. I needed to go to this dance!

And so it was that my younger sister, at my request,

taught me to dance—a little. She graciously taught me two of her "combinations." Two rather simple little sets of steps that she made up and coordinated to fit in with her many other steps. Two simple sets of movements that, believe it or not, I could easily do while Chuckie did his own combination. However, I could only do these two specific combinations, and once they were finished, well, so was I. This was a dilemma because while the combinations were great the first time and maybe even the second, they lost their charm when repeated over and over again. It took a lot of thought to figure out a solution to this puzzle, but once again, Chuckie took charge of the situation and devised a plan.

On the night of the dance, there I was. Chuckie and I parted company as soon as we arrived. We were now crowded into Jerry Holt's basement with a mixture of sweaty junior and senior high students. I was already sweaty myself, and had a very dry mouth. I felt my heart rate increase. I'm sure that many others were as anxious as I was, but somehow I was confident that all of them could DANCE! One lone, dim bulb was the only light, for which I was grateful. This meant I could move around and talk to my girlfriends and not be seen by everyone. And I could keep an eye out for Chuckie and Clyde while still using other people as camouflage. I had taken great care in applying my eyebrows. But thinking about this made me even more anxious, wondering if I had interpreted Clyde's reaction incorrectly, so I tried to concentrate on my upcoming performance. Bookworm or not, even Clyde could dance, according to Chuckie, but maybe he had just said that to convince me to try his stupid "plan." My anxiety increased. What if Judy's combination wasn't enough? And even if it was enough, would I be able to remember it? And Chuckie, would he remember that this was the only combination I knew? He couldn't try to do anything else—break out on his own and do something fancy!

I went to his side to remind him of this for the second time. He responded impatiently, as only a big brother can.

"I know what I have to do. You just remember what you have to do. We won't do it at the very beginning of the song; the floor will be crowded so you can do just about anything and no one will notice. But we do have to dance a little bit before it happens, remember? Now take it easy, and I'll come and get you when it's time."

I tried to hide behind others most of the time while I waited. I pretended to talk with some of my girlfriends and only really made myself visible when the slow songs were playing. Everyone knew how to dance to slow songs. As my dear brother had advised me, "If you have a problem, just lean into whoever you're dancing with. They'll love it!"

The basement where the dance was being held was now more crowded and getting warmer by the second. Maybe I could just say that I was too hot to dance. No, Chuckie would kill me. But, before too long, or maybe just in time, I saw Chuckie heading toward me across the crowded basement and I knew it was time. Some of our mutual friends parted to let Chuckie through. I heard someone say, "No, that's Nancy, not Judy." I should have answered, "You're out of luck tonight, buddy!"

I was so nervous that I felt faint. There was a loud buzzing in my ears, and I felt as if I was having a hard time breathing. Very soon Chuckie and I were dancing with the group, but soon, there was just Chuckie and me. Me trying to smile, and Chuckie with a big smile saying not yet...not yet. And then it was time. We did our first combination, which must have been okay, because there were cries of A-L-R-I-G-H-T! A few more regular steps and then our combination again. More approval. And then it happened. I cried out in pain and dropped to the floor, holding my ankle.

"I turned you too fast," said Chuckie, as people gathered around to help me.

"I'm okay," I assured everyone. "I just need to sit down, and maybe no more dancing tonight."

Various classmates helped me to a chair, and Clyde was among them.

"Go finish dancing," I bravely said to Chuckie. "You can teach our step to someone else. It's okay."

Chuckie, appearing somewhat reluctant, although only I knew he really wasn't, returned to the dance floor, and others, seeing that I was okay, returned also. The party was once again in full swing. I tearfully apologized to Clyde. "That's what you get when you want to show off," I said. He comforted me very sweetly and we spent the rest of the evening together.

It was one of the best parties I ever attended. I could sit back and enjoy the party with no expectations from anyone, including myself. When it ended, I was driven home in Clyde's brother's car. After all, I couldn't very well walk on a sore ankle. That was the night of my first and only dancing debut, and also my first kiss!

Nancy McKeever

The Drummer

My big brother Chuckie was only two years older than me, but I thought him wiser than his years and loved knowing that I had a big brother to protect me from the many unknowns of high school.

Tall, six-foot-four, and gangly, he had long thin arms and legs that could have made him move awkwardly, but this was not the case. He moved fluidly, limbs akimbo, like a giant praying mantis moving easily along a leaf. Judy called him "Bug."

Musical and manic, he dashed energetically around our apartment and was always drumming—on tabletops, books, walls, and the backs of his ever-exasperated sisters. He loved music and loved to dance. Using me as his partner, he would spend hours practicing his steps before attending a party. He told me, "We'll look almost like a professional team, but no one will know that we've practiced. Think of all the boys watching you!"

Though slim in build, he had full cheeks with high cheekbones, and like his five siblings, had a gap between his two front teeth. Chuckie loved to laugh and had a loud, infectious laugh, which made it hard to stay angry with him under any circumstances, even when he was using his fingers to drum on your back.

Growing up in the poor section of Homewood-Brushton in Pittsburgh, we lived on a tight budget that did not allow for anything beyond the bare necessities of life. This made it difficult for Chuckie, who always wanted to be dressed in the latest styles. While we suffered with hand-me-downs and last year's fashions, Chuckie set about creating a new wardrobe for himself. This was a time when khaki pants were all the rage. My brother, who had his own sense of fashion, bought five pairs of khakis with money from his paper route. He then bought Rit dye in blue, green, black, and gray and proceeded to dye four pairs of pants. After dyeing them, he starched and ironed them almost as neatly as my mother would have done. When finished, he had a week's worth of clothing and never had to wear the same color pants twice. Even as an adult, he hated to wear the same outfit more than once during a week and looked elegant every day that he went to work as Western Regional Director for the Xerox Corporation.

Music and rhythm were an important part of his life from a young age. He went from drumming on his sisters to joining the band in junior high school. He was seldom seen without drumsticks in his hand. He remained in the band throughout junior high, and in high school he joined the marching band and the orchestra. In the orchestra, his favorite drum was the timpani, and in the marching band, the bass drum. The band, he thought, was a much more sophisticated group. First of all, he got to wear a uniform, and what fine uniforms they were. The uniform jackets were navy blue with gold braid on the shoulders. Two rows of large gold buttons adorned the jacket, and the waist was cinched by a white belt with a gold buckle. The outfit was completed by navy blue pants with a gold stripe down the side, white buck shoes, and a navy blue cap also decorated in gold braid. He cut a fine figure in this outfit, and I envied his place in the band.

Uniforms were not worn on a daily basis, but saved for special events like concerts, football games, and parades. We were a small African American and Italian community, so it was a small parade with the only music provided by the Westinghouse High School Marching Band. The parade route started at the library and wound its way up Homewood Avenue, ending at the Homewood Cemetery. On parade day, breakfast would be a hurried affair because we wanted to get in place early to save "our spot." The spot had to be just right. Not at the very beginning of the parade or at the end, but right in the middle, when everyone was at their very best. We would tell Chuckie, "We'll be in front of the bakery" or "We'll be across from the butcher shop!" In this way, he would know we were there and feel our support. We, in turn, would get to proudly yell, "That's my brother!"

One year, we waited eagerly as the parade snaked its way up Homewood Avenue and heard the loud boom, boom, boom, boom, of the big bass drum. There was a wide assortment of marchers, from Mrs. Patterson's ballet school with little girls in pink tutus to the serious-looking local chapter of the Elks. Most important to us, however, was the Westinghouse High School Marching Band. And here they came, buttons and belt buckles shining in the bright sunlight, white bucks all in step, looking like one giant centipede making its way down the street. As I looked down the right side of the line of the band, I could see Chuckie, a head taller than anyone else, with his big bass drum strapped to his waist. His long arms flew out to the side with each boom of the drum, the drumstick coming very close to the spectators who lined the street. It was as if the boom of his drum was driving the entire parade. Boom! Boom! Boom! He was almost to us, and yes, he saw us and smiled his gap-toothed smile. "Chuckie! Chuckie!" we screamed and clapped our hands proudly. Closer and closer he came, and although I wanted to reach out and touch him, I knew I didn't dare. There seemed to be a twinkle in his eyes. And then, as he reached us, and while continuing to mark out the pace with his left hand, my brother reached over and with his right hand tapped me lightly on the head twice with his drumstick! Never breaking his stride, and never missing a beat. The spectators closest to me laughed, cheered, and clapped as my brother continued to make his way with the band up Homewood Avenue, back straight and eyes forward.

I was questioned repeatedly by other spectators: "Are you the girl that the drummer tapped on the head? Did it hurt? Oh, he's your brother!" Then we all laughed together. I felt like the prom queen. I continued to watch the long serpentine line move up the street. As the band moved farther away and other parade participants passed by, I continued to watch my brother for as long as I could see his right arm jut smartly out with each syncopated beat of the big bass drum.

Look Toward the Future

"Shirley Elizabeth Flurry," she would say when asked her name; her enunciation and diction always sharp and clear. We called her Snip, and there were several family versions of how she obtained this nickname. One story was that when she was born, she had just a "snip of a nose." Another story described her as being "just a snip of a thing when she was a baby." No matter, Snip was who she was to the family. Blessed with a lovely speaking voice, she was an excellent student and prided herself on always being grammatically correct. She used to coach me, saying, "When you get to high school and the teacher asks you to do something, you must always say, 'Yes, I shall.'" I didn't quite understand then (nor do I now) the rules that govern the proper use of *shall* versus *will*, but I didn't question for a second that she was absolutely correct.

I loved all my siblings most of the time—even my older brothers, who teased us mercilessly with spiders and grasshoppers and other crawling species and draped their sweaty basketball T-shirts over our heads—but Snip, seven years older than me, was my role model in every way and I wanted so much to be just like her.

I thought Snip was beautiful at age eighteen with

her smooth, coffee-colored skin and high cheekbones. She had dark brown hair, which she wore parted on the left side with one curl that hung delicately over her right eyebrow She reminded me of Elizabeth Taylor in the movie *A Place in the Sun*.

At age eleven, I was tall and scrawny, had reddish-brown hair, wore Board of Education-sponsored glasses, which were functional but certainly not stylish, and sported orthopedic shoes that looked better suited for someone of my mother's age. My sister, on the other hand, was beautiful, curvaceous, and stylish, and she wore penny loafers with an actual penny in them. Oh, how I wanted to trade places with her. Sometimes, when she was being especially generous, she would allow me to sit with her and her friends as they discussed hairstyles, boys, music, boys, clothes, and more boys. I would watch her carefully as she got dressed to go to a party and as she applied the minimal amount of makeup our father would allow us to wear, and then topped it off with my mother's Royal Purple lipstick.

Being the oldest girl brought with it a great deal of responsibility. My mother worked every day, and my father was not present for weeks at a time. This left Snip "in charge," a position that often led to her being at odds with the rest of us, which sometimes resulted in her being punitive and angry in her efforts to maintain control over her five younger siblings. Her decisions determined our daily activities, and she always seemed so sure of herself. She never showed any doubt or vulnerability.

    Snip worked hard all through her junior high and high school years with the hope that she would someday go to college. She was determined to do whatever was necessary to escape our poverty-dominated upbringing and create a life that more closely resembled her idea of the American Dream. A challenging but fulfilling job, a happy marriage, children, and home ownership were all included in her dreams of the future. When the announcement was made revealing that she was class valedictorian, everyone was ecstatic. What an honor! All her work had paid off and she was about to start her promising future. It meant, of course, that a speech had to be written. I remember her laboring diligently over her speech with the assistance of her English teacher, Miss Edgar, a large, forbidding-looking woman who wore thick, round wire-rimmed glasses that made her piercing eyes seem even larger. She had the smell of mothballs about her, wore what appeared to be thick support hose, and had untidy hair that lightly dusted her shoulders with dandruff. Miss Edgar was a demanding but knowledgeable teacher, and they worked together on it for hours. At last, the speech was ready and its title was "Look to the Future." Next came the task of memorizing it for the big night. Snip asked me to help her with this, and I felt very special to be the one chosen for this task. We spent many evenings in our cramped, crowded kitchen; me following along word for word while Snip had to remember not only the words to her speech but also to stand tall and to speak slowly and distinctly. During this time, she continued to talk of the possibility of furthering her education.

Although there was certainly no money in the household, it seemed impossible to me that someone this talented would not be offered some type of scholarship as a reward for her efforts. Miss Edgar attempted to find financial assistance for her.

Graduation night came and Snip recited her speech perfectly: standing tall, hands clasped loosely in front of her, pausing at just the right moments, and emphasizing the correct points. I had practically memorized the speech with her by that time and felt proud that I had in some way helped her accomplish this goal. Her speech was a success and gave me one more detail to add to my list of "How to be like Snip."

Though she tried, Miss Edgar was unable to obtain financial assistance for my sister, and her dreams of college were soon just that—dreams. My mother understood Snip's wish to do more, but my father could focus only on the fact that she was out of school and could now get a job and contribute to the household finances. So that is what my intelligent, beautiful sister did. Instead of going off to college, where she could bask in academia, where she could find herself and grow, she took a job as a nurse's aide. Married at age twenty, she eventually managed to attend night school at Trade Tech in Pittsburgh. While working, and caring for a husband and three children, my sister gradually moved into management-type jobs with more responsibility. She took advantage of all the classes offered at her various jobs, still seeking any educational opportunities and moving steadily up the management ladder.

Snip is now retired from her county job as supervisor of the Disability Unit. Five years prior to her retirement, still in her big sister role, she discussed with me her "five-year plan" so that she could retire and live well. She advised me to create my own plan. She successfully carried hers out. Currently, she lives contentedly in a home that is paid for, drives a car that is paid for, and with her savings, county retirement, her husband's pension, and Social Security has no money worries. She and I have talked about her status in life and her ability to successfully achieve these things without a college degree. During a conversation with the four sisters together for the first time in seven years, we reminisced about our childhood. Snip once again discussed the unfairness of missing out on an opportunity for college due to our childhood circumstances. She started out in anger, but gradually became more subdued. She ended the discussion by saying wistfully, sounding more like an eighteen-year-old than an eighty-year-old, the longing still painfully raw in her voice, "I wonder how my life would have been different if I had been able to go to college. Somehow, I still believe I could have accomplished more."

I found myself saddened and tearful. It was only then that I fully understood that she had been given too much responsibility far too soon. She had looked to the future, but the future had not cooperated.

The Price of Silence

1.

Always focused on appearances and what she considered "proper behavior," my father's sister insisted that we call her Aunt Elizabeth, not the less formal Aunt Betty. When she married at age forty-five much to everyone's surprise, including hers, it was of course assumed that her husband would be called Uncle Walter. A big, burly construction worker, Walter seemed nice enough to me. He called us all "sweetie" and didn't seem to mind three giggling girls—me, Judy, and Mimsi—taking over the guest bedroom on our frequent weekend visits to their home.

They lived in a house in the section of Homewood that bordered on Wilkinsburg, Pennsylvania. We lived in Homewood, a poor, mostly Black neighborhood; Wilkinsburg was predominantly middle-class and white. We considered their sturdy brick house a mansion compared to the dilapidated tenement in which we lived. They lived on the second floor, which had two bedrooms, a living room, a dining room, a kitchen, and a bathroom. They rented out the first-floor apartment to a single older woman. The basement had been converted to a small hair salon where Aunt Elizabeth spent many late hours as a successful hairdresser. Sometimes she would do our hair, and the payment extracted was the completion of various household chores.

Having no children of her own, Aunt Elizabeth made a conscious effort to spend time with us. She introduced us to the members of her bridge club and attempted to teach me how to play bridge, as she felt this was one of the attributes of being "a lady." I was tall, thin, shy, and quiet at the time, and maybe she thought I needed instruction. She also had us "dress nicely" and accompany her on Sundays when she made her "pop calls." These were short visits to briefly check in with her friends, maybe have a cup of tea, and then move on to the next friend. At ages eight, six, and three, we had no interest in spending time learning how to play bridge, pop-calling, or being ladies, but both my parents encouraged us, verbally and nonverbally, to be nice to Aunt Elizabeth. It was well known that she often helped us out financially, and as any poor person can tell you, debts are often collected in a myriad of ways. So we spent time with Aunt Elizabeth and Uncle Walter, and I always felt that for a few hours on those weekends, she could pretend she had her own real family.

Because I was the oldest, Uncle Walter said I was " special," and he would give me the change from his pockets when he arrived home from work on Friday evenings, instructing me to divide it between the three of us and reminding me to take a little extra for my special self. Although he seemed less sophisticated in every way compared to Aunt Elizabeth with her weekly bridge club, her participation in bridge tournaments in an effort to raise her standing in the bridge community, and her weekly book club that included the author Frances J. Barnes. Frances wrote poetry and prose and in 1977 published the book *LOVE: From Black Men to Black Women*. (Aunt Elizabeth treasured her signed copy of this book and gave it to me many years ago.) I never saw Walter pick up a book or even read the newspaper, but she seemed happy in her life with him.

One Saturday afternoon, a perfect Pittsburgh summer day, sunny and warm but not too humid, Aunt Elizabeth, Judy, Mimsi, and I were in her modest backyard, where there was actual grass as opposed to the dusty dirt-covered ground that we were used to at home. Aunt Elizabeth was preparing a barbecue for us. The smell of grilling hot dogs wafted through the air and reminded us that breakfast had been many hours earlier. Grilled hot dogs stuffed with cheese and wrapped in bacon were something she had introduced to us that we actually enjoyed. This unbelievable treat would be accompanied by corn on the cob, cucumber and tomato salad, fresh-squeezed lemonade, and a surprise dessert, which she had not yet revealed.

Nancy McKeever

We were busily shucking corn while Aunt Elizabeth sliced tomatoes and cucumbers for the salad. "Nancy, go tell your Uncle Walter that we'll be ready to eat in forty-five minutes," my aunt said to me. The sunny day darkened, as did my mood. I was reluctant to face Uncle Walter. He had gotten into the habit of crawling into our bedroom on all fours. Circling the bed we all shared, he passed Judy, who slept closest to the door, and Mimsi, who slept in the middle, and made his way around to my side, where I slept with my back facing the wall. There was just enough room for him to sit between the bed and the wall. I held my breath, wondering if he would just sit there for a while as he usually did, pajamas rustling slightly, and then after uttering a soft grunt, crawl slowly back around the bed and out of the room. The previous night had been different. I heard a soft scratching noise as his huge calloused hand slid between the sheets. I tried very hard to remain still, as if I were sleeping, but was surprised that he could not feel the trembling of my body. I felt that same hand slowly work its way up my leg like some scaly, rough-skinned snake slithering toward its prey. When his hand reached the hem of my thin cotton nightgown, I began kicking and thrashing around, calling out as if I were having a nightmare. My heart pounded rapidly and my movements startled my sisters, who began to move around also. This seemed to interrupt his actions at least for that moment. Waiting patiently until we all settled again, Walter stealthily made his way back around the bed and out of the door. Aunt Elizabeth, two floors below in the basement doing hair, remained unaware of his activity.

I had seen him at breakfast in the morning and again as he was on his way downstairs to fix a leak in the shop when he stopped and we had a brief interaction. Looking pleased that we were alone, and with a slight smile on his face, he said, "I have a secret to tell you, but you have to promise not to tell anyone. I'm only telling you because you're special, you know. I'll tell you later." He disappeared quickly down the stairs as I stood there trembling and shaken, with no idea as to what I should do but knowing that I wanted no "secret" from him.

Now I had to go into the house and actually seek him out. I couldn't tell Aunt Elizabeth no without an explanation, and how could I even begin to describe Uncle Walter's frequent forays into our bedroom at night? With my heart beating rapidly, I made my way to the back door and entered the kitchen.

"Uncle Walter," I called loudly. "We'll be eating in forty-five minutes. Okay?" Receiving no answer and reluctant to go down the hall to their bedroom, I called again.

"Uncle Walter, did you hear me?" At that point he came out of the bedroom. His pants were unzipped. I moved backward toward the kitchen door.

"Wait, sweetie," he said, as he continued to advance toward me. "I wanted to tell you a secret, remember? Your Aunt Elizabeth and I are planning to buy you all a television for Christmas. Wouldn't you like that? But remember, it's a secret and you can't tell anyone, even your Aunt Elizabeth, that I told you. Your brothers and sisters will be surprised and you, my special girl, will be the only one that knows ahead of time."

A television! I couldn't believe it. We thought we were the only family in the world without a TV. All our friends had one, but it was an expense we couldn't afford. I imagined Chuckie (my ten-year-old brother), Judy, and Mimsi waking up on Christmas morning to see a TV sitting under the mantel where the little heater now sat. Christmas gifts usually consisted of socks, underwear, and one small toy or doll. But a TV! I could see us sitting shoulder to shoulder watching...anything!

Uncle Walter moved closer while I was caught up in my TV fantasy. With one swift movement, he grasped both of my skinny eight-year-old arms with one huge rough hand and swung my body around until my back was pressed firmly against the refrigerator. He grasped my left hand and quickly stuffed it into his unzipped pants, using it to stroke his erect penis. I remember thinking that his penis felt so smooth in comparison to his scratchy hands. I became lightheaded, my heart pounded, I hyperventilated. I could hear my sisters and Aunt Elizabeth laughing and talking in the backyard, but they seemed very far away, and the world appeared blurry and fuzzy around the edges. I made no sound, hoping frantically that this waking nightmare would end.

"Nancy, ask your Uncle Walter to bring the baked beans and come out in a half hour." I heard my Aunt Elizabeth's voice as it cut through the fog of my terror. Uncle Walter let me go. I made my escape and ran quickly through the back door and out into the sunshine of that "special" summer day.

As summer evolved into fall and Christmas neared, Uncle Walter's behavior escalated. He began to call me into his bedroom while Mimsi and Judy watched *Tom and Jerry* or *Yogi Bear* on TV and while Aunt Elizabeth was busy in her basement salon. I couldn't help but wonder if our television would be as nice as theirs and if I would be able to watch it without thinking of Uncle Walter. With him clad only in his brown and gold bathrobe, we would sit with our backs to the door so as not to be seen if one of my sisters burst through the bedroom door. I would stare out the bedroom window overlooking the backyard as he guided my hand over his penis, stroking it again and again. Sometimes he would use the hem of his bathrobe to wipe the stickiness off the palm of my hand. The yard was closed in on one side by a metal fence with big round balls spaced at intervals approximately eight to ten inches apart. I would start at the far left and slowly count those balls: one...two...three. At the far right, I would then count backwards: fourteen...thirteen...twelve. Sometimes the numbers didn't always come out correctly.

We got our TV on Christmas Eve, delivered by my father with orders to use Aunt Sarah's phone (our apartments were joined by a common bathroom) to call Aunt Elizabeth immediately and thank her. We were able to do this without any contact with Uncle Walter. We were allowed to stay up late that night to watch TV and begged to stay up even later. Everyone assumed that they knew why I was crying when we reluctantly crawled into bed.

2.

When I was almost ten years old, I enlisted the help of my sister Judy to convince my mother to make other arrangements for our weekends. Judy, younger than me but always more outspoken, was a willing participant even though she remained unaware of Uncle Walter's behavior.

I introduced the subject in this way. "Momma, when we go to Aunt Elizabeth's, she washes our hair and puts it in all these ugly plaits and we have to stay inside until she finishes all her customers on Friday and Saturday. We can't even go across the street to the corner store with our hair like that! It's like being in jail!"

Judy chimed in. "She treats us just like slaves, Momma! She always has a sink piled full of dishes, beds to make, and we even have to dust down her steps on our hands and knees. I hate going there!"

My usually unflappable mother sighed, maybe thinking of what could be a difficult conversation with my father about his sainted sister. "I'll talk to your father tonight, but right now I'm going to sit down. Nancy, you and Chuckie clean up the kitchen."

"What's wrong with going there?" whispered my twelve-year-old brother Chuckie, when my mother had left the room. Already tall for his age, he was lean and lanky with ears that stuck out just a little too far from his head. "She fixes you anything you want to eat, Walter gives you money, and you get to sleep in that big bed with no bedbugs! You guys aren't the ones that have to bring her a paper or walk through the snow to get a stupid cat off her porch because she's afraid of cats! That's always me! Stop complaining!"

"And you don't have Walter stuffing your hand in his pants and rubbing his dick, now do you?" I spat back at him. And then I told him the whole story. I started sobbing, but yelled in shock and pain as Chuckie punched me solidly on the arm.

"What's going on in there?" my mother called from the next room.

"Nothing," we said in unison.

"Why didn't you tell me before? I'm going to kill him! What about Judy and Mimsi? Them too?"

I shook my head no.

"I'll take care of it. Don't worry about it, and keep your mouth shut!"

"But what will you do? How will you take care of it? He's a big man!"

"Just be quiet and don't ask so many questions!"

We finished cleaning the kitchen in silence with me being sure I was asking my tall jug-eared twelve-year-old brother to do the impossible.

Sometime during the following week, my father made a brief visit to the apartment to deliver a message to all of us including my mother.

"Everybody be careful out there. Some gang beat up Walter, and Liz had to take him to the emergency room at Pittsburgh Hospital. Probably some of those rough Negroes from The Hill."

The Hill was an even poorer section of Pittsburgh than Homewood, where we lived.

"Yes, Daddy," we all said.

Later, Chuckie whispered, "The 'gang' was me, Ronnie, Gerald, Bobby, and Randy. We beat him up and told him to stay away from little girls or we'd kill him!"

"But what if...."

"I don't want to talk about it! If he tries something again, tell me, but I don't think he will."

My brother, his two best friends, and my two cousins, all between the ages of eleven and twelve, had come to my defense. I kept waiting for repercussions from the incident, but none were forthcoming. The TV that had been received so joyously that Christmas by everyone except me had come at a price that had been far too steep.

3.

After that, we saw Elizabeth and Walter infrequently over the years—only at family reunions, weddings, or funerals. I got married, had two daughters, and then separated from my husband. In my thirties, I was living platonically with my best friend, Esther, and her daughter, Heather. My daughters Stacey and Nancy Jean were eleven and six, and Heather was three. Occasionally, when I did see Elizabeth at family gatherings, she would mention that the girls were welcome to visit anytime. I ignored her offers.

Answering the phone one afternoon, I was surprised

to hear Elizabeth's voice. Speaking in her usual affected way, she asked about me and then inquired about "the girls."

"You know when I say 'the girls' I mean Heather also," she said.

Once I assured her that we were all well, she went on to explain the exact nature of her call.

"I didn't see you over the holidays, but I bought the girls some Christmas gifts. I thought this weekend they could come for dinner, spend the night, and open presents the next day."

"No, Elizabeth," I said.

"You know, Nancy, you're being very selfish," she said angrily. "I've wanted the girls to visit and you always say no. I know you're their mother, but you must allow them to spend time with other people. You and your sisters spent plenty of time here when you were young and had fun and I don't understand why you say no about your daughters and Heather."

If she said anything else after that, I didn't hear it. My voice got louder, my heart pounded as if someone had taken a hammer to my chest, and I saw the world through a red curtain of rage.

"You want to know why they can't come, Elizabeth? It's because of Walter! Walter, who used to creep into our room on all fours and masturbate beside the bed! Walter, who put his hands under the sheets while we slept! My daughters will never spend a night in that house!"

"I don't believe you. Why are you saying these terrible things?"

"Walter, who repeatedly took me into your bedroom dressed only in his robe and used my hand to stroke his penis. All this while you were downstairs in that shop doing everyone's hair except ours!"

Click. She hung up the phone. Enraged, I called her back.

"Damn it, Elizabeth, don't hang up on me! Did you know? While you were down in your shop, did you know what he was doing?"

"I won't listen to this! You have to stop now!"

She ended the call with a phrase I had heard many times before when I was young.

"I'm going to tell your father!"

Click. She hung up again.

I called back a third time. By this time, I was in the center of my bed, on my knees screaming obscenities, spittle on my chin and no sense of where I was anymore, until I turned and saw, standing open-mouthed in the doorway, Esther and the three girls.

"Take them out, Esther. Please take them out!"

When I had hung up for the third and final time, my last words of "I hope you do tell my father" reverberated in the air.

I approached my next weekly visit with my parents with a mixture of trepidation but also hope that this long-kept secret might finally be revealed. Had Elizabeth told my father about our conversations? Did she tell him what I said about Walter? What was his response then, and what would he say to me now? Had he in turn told my mother? Entering my parents' house, my daughters were greeted loudly by Pa-pa, as they called my father.

"Look who's here, Sue," my father called to my mother.

"Grandma, we're here and we brought you pictures to hang on the refrigerator!"

As the girls made their way to the kitchen, my father hesitated in the front doorway.

"I hear you and your Aunt Betty had a falling-out."

"Yes, we did," I said, turning to face him directly.

After another moment of hesitation, he continued matter-of-factly, "It'll work out."

He then closed the door behind himself and left.

I stood there stunned. *It'll work out?* What the hell did that even mean? I still had no answers to the many questions that swirled in my brain. I felt disappointed, relieved, and angry all at the same time.

Entering the kitchen, I was greeted with a warm hug and kiss by my mother. I knew I couldn't bring up the topic of Walter today, and maybe never after all this time. I didn't know who I was protecting by continuing to carry this secret alone.

4.

The room vibrated with a low-pitched hum punctuated occasionally by louder voices as old friends greeted each other. Some of our family members sat in a makeshift semicircle, talking softly. It was March of 1998, and I was attending my father's wake in Pittsburgh. We were sitting far enough away from the casket to allow visitors to view the body, but close enough to ensure that my mother was easily accessible to family and friends who were there to offer their condolences. On this third and final day of the wake, I sat quietly with my mother and aunts, as they carried on their usual storytelling as a way to keep close daily tabs on each other's lives and those of their neighbors. I heard my mother repeating again how she had allowed my father, on the day he died, to seduce her into cooking his favorite, completely forbidden lunch of fried potatoes, ham, and biscuits made from scratch. Lunch finished, he went upstairs for his daily nap and never woke up. I sat there quietly lulled by the familiar rise and fall of these voices that I had heard all my life. Each one distinctive, yet somehow the same. My Aunt Sarah, the oldest of the living sisters, sat regally in her chair with her ever-present Kool cigarette in one hand and a small tin ashtray in the other. She was tall and thin with dark mahogany-colored skin and carried herself like an African queen. She ignored my Aunt Clara's request to "put that damn thing out," maybe because Clara also smoked whenever and wherever she wanted. In fact, all four of my mother's sisters smoked, drank, and swore like lumberjacks, although my mother did none of these. Clara, two years younger than Sarah, was my favorite aunt and I think my mother's favorite sister. We spent plenty of time at her home when we were young because she and my mother (each with six children) shared babysitting duties as they cleaned houses to put food on the table. We used to beg to go visit her every possible weekend in the relaxed atmosphere of her crowded but spotless home situated in the Black section of Wilkinsburg. Virgie, my mother's sister-in-law, was also included in the group. She was short, round, and soft-spoken and was liked by all and considered one of the sisters.

Wanting to see where my siblings were and if we could diplomatically end this last evening, I moved slightly to the left to ease away from the group undetected. It was at this point that I heard my Aunt Sarah refer to "that damn Walter! That man was a bastard if ever there was one!"

Elizabeth and Walter had died within a year of each

other. I had not seen them in many years prior to their death. For a moment, it was 1950 and I was eight years old again. Which Walter was she referring to? The Walter who crawled into our room at night and masturbated beside our bed? The Walter who, with the promise of a TV for Christmas, used my hand to touch his penis? Whose wife, many years later, dared to invite my daughters to spend the night in the same house and bed where he had traumatized me? That Walter? Why were they even talking about him?

"That damn Walter," Sarah continued. "He told me one time 'I'd never look at a woman like you 'cause I don't like skinny Black women.' I told him to kiss my skinny Black ass!"

"Johnny [my Aunt Clara's husband] told him he was going to shoot him if he didn't stop touching me," chimed in Aunt Clara. "I don't know who he thought would want him besides Elizabeth, and we know she was just desperate to get a husband."

Virgie, in her soft voice, added, "At least you never had to live there. When Flurry [her husband, my father's brother] got his first teaching job, we lived there for six months. When I would come out of the room in the morning, no matter how quiet I tried to be, he would open the bedroom door and stand there with an open robe and sometimes totally naked. He told me I could go in that room any time I want to. He was a nasty man. I never told Flurry, I just said we had to move as soon as possible. We left there in six months."

My whole body reacted to what I was hearing. My breathing became very shallow, like when I tried not to breathe when I was young pretending to be asleep with Walter crouched at the bedside. My legs became tight, the way they feel when tensing, getting ready to flee.

"He was a bully," my mother finally said.

I had been waiting for her to add to the conversation.

"I would be walking home after work and we would both be on Oakwood Street, sometimes right in front of their house. He would walk straight into me until we touched or I had to step to the side in the dirt. "Thurston sho is a lucky man," he would say with his phony Southern accent. "Leave me alone or I'll tell Thurston that you tried to push me around," I told him. "Just jokin' Susie," he would say. But we both knew it was no joke! I did tell Thurston, and he said he talked to both Walter and Elizabeth. All I know is that he stopped."

I sat there stunned and confused. They knew. They knew what he was like and still they allowed us to go there. Surely everyone was aware of his behavior. My mother and my Aunt Clara talked every day about everything, and I found it hard to believe that the topic of Walter did not arise. Did she think we were safe because we were children? Oh Momma, how could you?

For that night, and many nights after, this painful, torturous thought occupied my mind. At times I would think such a scenario impossible and at others I'd be convinced there was no way they could not know. I didn't know if my mother was aware of what she had allowed, and never confronted her about this issue, something I regret to this day. I did discuss it with my sisters. They were totally unaware of Walter's behavior and had no idea of the events that occurred in or out of that bedroom.

"You should have told us," Judy said. "We could have at least screamed or something. We would have fought him!"

I was eight years old. It never crossed my mind.

Do I think about this all the time? No. But this incident, and its impact over almost seventy years, continues to affect me. I remain a light sleeper, not disturbed by light or noise, but immediately awakened by what I feel is a change in the air current in the room, as if some unwanted entity is disturbing the atmosphere. I also do not move much once in bed. Awake or asleep, I am very still, so that at times even my partner asks, "Are you awake?" Are these responses connected to Walter? I don't know.

What I do know is that a secret such as this is a

heavy burden for one to bear alone. But it's a burden whose weight can be lightened even seventy years later by bringing it out of the darkness of shame.

Nancy at Capping Ceremony

NURSE NANCY

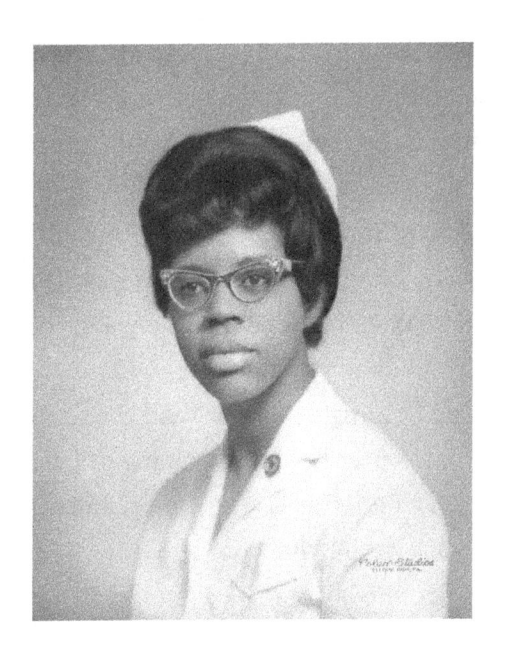

The Postman

I heard Clarence's familiar whistle before he arrived at our house with the daily mail. It was a tuneless whistle, the same notes every day, familiar in that it belonged to him, but the tune itself was unrecognizable. Clarence was our postman and had been for the past ten years. He was a short, stocky man with an energetic stride. He had a dimple in his left cheek, an affable manner, and a quick "How's the day?" for everyone. Every family on our one-block street knew and liked him, and you could easily hear him as he made his way from one row house to the next.

I heard him first at Miss Allen's house. She lived two doors away from us. I heard the clunk, clunk of her metal mailbox as he deposited her mail. Both Miss Allen and her mailbox were getting older, although she appeared to be holding up better than the box. It had a screw missing from one side, so it hung at a downward angle like a melting letter L whose horizontal arm was sliding slowly downhill. You would hear one clunk when Clarence opened the box and a second when he actually deposited the mail and closed the lid.

Then I heard him talking to Betty, our next-door neighbor. "Hi Betty, how's the day?

"It's hot, but at least the humidity is down," she said. "Would you like some ice water?"

Come on, Clarence, I thought impatiently. *Bring the mail!* My impatience had to do with the fact that I was waiting for the results of my RN licensing examination. The exam was the culmination of years of work. I had gone to Harrisburg, Pennsylvania, six weeks prior to take the exam and fervently hoped I would pass. If I failed, it would mean taking a three-month break before I could try again. Then another six weeks of waiting for results. I would not be issued a license, nor could I work, until I achieved a passing score in all exam categories. This was important!

Next door, I heard Clarence graciously accept Betty's offer of a drink and a few seconds later heard him utter a satisfied "A-h-h-h." After telling her goodbye, he stepped lightly from her worn steps to mine.

"Hi Nancy, how's the day? Looks like an exciting letter has arrived for you. Return address is Board of Registered Nursing. Know you've been waiting for this!"

Of course he knew. I thought back over the past three and a half years as Clarence, like a member of the family, had followed my progress in becoming a registered nurse.

It was Clarence who had brought the letter with the news of a scholarship from the Jewish Women's Auxiliary

League of the Liliane S. Kaufmann School of Nursing of Montefiore Hospital in Pittsburgh. I had been awarded a three-year scholarship to nursing school, which included both books and uniforms. It was a scary and exciting time of my life, and although I lived in the nurses' residence, I still came home some weekends or occasionally brought a friend home for a weekday dinner. I only saw Clarence on school breaks, but he always made some comment to my mother when my grades arrived in an envelope with Liliane S. Kaufmann as the return address. According to my mother, Clarence would say "Conemaugh Street will have its own nurse someday."

"Thanks, Clarence," I said as I grabbed the mail and headed back into my house.

"Wait a minute!" he said. "Don't I get to hear the news too?"

I hesitated. I wasn't sure if I wanted to share the news, favorable or unfavorable, with anyone. I had imagined opening the letter in the privacy of an empty house, where I could laugh and dance like a whirling dervish if I'd passed or storm and cry like a baby if I'd failed.

"Clarence," I said, "I don't know if I want to open it around anyone. What if I didn't pass?"

He did not respond immediately, but shrugged, moved his heavy bag from one shoulder to the other, and then said slowly, "Okay, then. Tell me tomorrow." Making a final adjustment to his bag, he stepped over the next set of steps to my neighbor's house. I ran inside, slamming the door, and tore at the official-looking envelope. Scarcely breathing, I scanned the letter quickly and saw the first word in the body of the letter: *Congratulations!* I had passed! Three years of hard work, terror, studying, laughing, and crying all summed up in one word. My license would be arriving within two weeks, according to the letter. I already knew where I wanted to work. Western Psychiatric Institute and Clinic, a comprehensive inpatient and outpatient evaluation and treatment center for people with psychiatric issues. It was the facility where I had done my three-month psychiatric rotation, and I'd promised the full-time staff I would return once I was licensed. Now, I could.

Now that the initial excitement was over, I realized that I *did* want to share my momentous news. Who could I tell? My family was either at work or school, but this news had to be shared with someone now. Someone who had accompanied me on my journey, starting with the notification of my scholarship, through my initial admission, my capping ceremonies, the wait for grades, my graduation at the Rodef Shalom Temple, and now this. I wasn't sure if this was the last step of my journey, or the first step of a new journey, but I knew of one other person who could bear witness to it all. With my letter in hand,

I flung open the front door and yelled, "Clarence, wait!"

Clarence was still next door talking to our neighbor, Leonard. He turned to me as I waved the letter excitedly in the air. One look at my huge grin and he said to Leonard in a proud, booming voice, "Leonard, Conemaugh Street may only be one block long, but I bet we're the only street that has its own private nurse!"

Had he purposely waited? I'll never know.

Big Girls Don't Cry

"You will not cry," Mrs. Wilkins said softly but firmly. She then repeated it: "You will not cry." Mrs. Wilkins was my clinical instructor in nursing school. She confronted me as I rushed tearfully from a patient room.

It was 1960, and I was in the second six months of my first year in nurses' training. Not yet in the program for a full twelve months, I hadn't gone through the capping ceremonies that would allow me to wear a small unadorned white nurse's cap and a white bib over my sky-blue uniform. In my second year, my cap would have one black band, and two bands in my third year.

In the 1960s, unlike today, there were still diploma schools available for you to obtain your RN license. Instead of pursuing a two-year AA degree or a four-year BS, as is the practice today, one had the option of attending a three-year program at a diploma school. These schools focused heavily on clinical experience, and you received much of your training under the close supervision of a clinical instructor.

We had two clinical instructors that year. Miss Frankel was tall and skinny, with straight blonde hair that always looked as if it could use a good brisk brushing. She gave the impression of flightiness, and with her slightly rumpled appearance and her casual approach, you would expect her to be less discerning on the unit, but she was sharp and had high expectations of her students. Our second instructor was Mrs. Wilkins. The personification of professionalism, she was a short, chubby Black woman who had a starched look about her, both in her dress and her demeanor. She wore her hair pulled back tightly in a bun and never seemed to have a hair out of place. She spoke slowly and distinctly with a slight Southern drawl and seemed to hear and see everything. Though each was demanding in her own way, they were both supportive and protective of the student nurses.

Being a first-year student, I spent my mornings on the clinical unit and my afternoons in the classroom. This meant being on the unit for report at 7 a.m. and receiving an assignment of one patient. The regular staff was always eager to have students so they could assign us those patients who were the most time-consuming, those who did not require technical expertise but needed total assistance with ADLs (activities of daily living) such as eating and bathing.

My assignment that morning was Mrs. M. She was a seventy-two-year-old white, widowed female who had been brought in with dehydration and other medical diagnoses. She was now more stable medically but was blind. She had difficulty hearing and required help eating, bathing, and getting out of bed to sit up in a chair. On my assignment sheet, the word *complete* was written next to her name, which let me know that she did nothing without assistance. I had three hours to help her brush her teeth, eat, and bathe. I then had to medicate her, administer eye drops, get her out of bed to sit in a chair, brush her hair, make her bed, and tidy up her room before filling out her chart for that day and getting to class.

Gathering all my needed equipment, I entered her room. I found Mrs. M burrowed deeply in her bed like a bear hibernating for the winter and "not ready" to be disturbed. With much encouragement, I got her to brush her teeth and prepare for breakfast. After making two trips to the kitchen to exchange things she did not like, I proceeded to feed her breakfast. This was a very slow process, with her complaining constantly about the temperature of the eggs, the consistency of the cereal, and the generally poor quality of hospital food. It didn't help that she wore ill-fitting dentures that further slowed the eating process.

Next came the bed bath, which was much simpler to do on Annie, the class dummy, than on Mrs. M. The dummy was quiet and cooperative, while my patient was complaintive and uncooperative. I took pains to change the water often so it would be warm, to keep her covered so she wouldn't get chilled, to dry her thoroughly and then apply lotion, and to give her a back rub before changing her into a clean gown. Getting her up into a chair was not easy, and she protested loudly. Since she had trouble hearing, she spoke in a loud voice and you could hear her protests echoing down the hall.

"I don't want to sit up. I'm still too tired. Slow down!"

Throughout all of these tasks, I was very aware of Mrs. Wilkins in the hallway as she used to patrol up and down the halls listening to our patient interactions. Were we engaged with the patient? Were we teaching them about nutrition and medication compliance? All of this was to be a part of our morning's work. The rooms all had saloon doors, and I could see Mrs. Wilkins' stubby brown legs, her white nylons, and her neat white nursing shoes as she walked back and forth in the hallway. I felt confident that I was doing a good job with a difficult patient. Time was passing, and I still had medications and charting to take care of before leaving for class. It was a cardinal sin to not complete an assignment. I would have to tell Mrs. Wilkins and then the charge nurse, and get disapproving looks from both!

The oral medications were simple; however, the patient was reluctant to take her eye drops because she said they burned. Previous nurses had charted about this, so I was prepared for her arguments. I persisted and was able to administer the eye drops correctly despite her reluctance.

With the patient out of bed, changing the sheets was easy and I made sure my corners were perfect. Mrs. M complained bitterly during her ordered fifteen minutes out of bed, and I tried my best to soothe her by asking about her daughter and her grandchildren. After the allotted out-of-bed time had elapsed, I assisted her back into bed. Positioning all five pillows to her specifications, I was almost home free. Tidying up the room took no time, and at last I felt free to go. I felt I had accomplished my assignment well, and both the patient and the room were neat and clean.

"Mrs. M., I'm leaving now. I hope the rest of your day goes well," I said to her.

"Thank you, dear," she said.

I thought to myself, *she can be nice!* And then it happened; then she said it. In a soft voice, almost as if she were talking to herself, she said, "At least they didn't send one of those niggers in here today."

I was stunned and couldn't say anything.

She went on, "I usually have one every day."

I said a hurried goodbye and rushed out of the room and ran directly into my clinical instructor, Mrs. Wilkins, our only Black instructor. I looked to her for some gesture of comfort because, after all, she had heard the entire conversation. However, instead of comfort, I received this reply: "You will not cry," she said harshly. "Go to the ladies' room and wash your face. Once you have done that, you must complete your charting and you will be finished for the day."

Wiping the tears from my eyes, I made my way to the nurses station to finish my charting and, not waiting for my classmates, left the unit and headed to class. I saw Mrs. Wilkins on the elevator but she said nothing, not that day or any day thereafter. In my remaining two and a half years of training, we never spoke of the incident again.

Nancy McKeever

The Kiss That Stopped Traffic

The telephone on the fifth floor of the nurses' residence rang as we were watching Dick Clark's *American Bandstand*. I was close to the end of my first year at the Liliane S. Kaufmann School of Nursing of Montefiore Hospital. Our usual routine after class and work was to watch TV and then proceed to the hospital cafeteria for dinner. With me and several other residents were my three best friends at the school: Marlene Daily, better known as Bone, Margaret Barynk, known as Peggy, and Susan Elek.

Bone was lanky and thin, had a tomboyish air about her, and was the smartest student in the class. She was always ready for an adventure. Peggy was short and stocky and had gone to high school with Bone. She was the Robin to Bone's Batman. Susan was an intense, often anxious young woman and was simply referred to as Elek. My last name was Flurry so my nickname was Flur. I was less adventurous than Bone, but she could usually convince me to join her in her antics. We all lived on the same floor in the residence and had the same classes.

"It's for you, Flur. It's our mom," said Bone. She said "our mom" because my mother had made the four of us dinner several times to give us a break from hospital food. I lived only a twenty-minute trolley ride from the school while Bone and Peggy lived more than twenty miles away in Tarentum, Pennsylvania, and Elek lived even farther away. I ran to answer the phone.

"Hi, Momma! How are you?"

She said in a mournful voice, "I never thought I'd see the day when my daughter would ignore me. I waved until my arm was tired, but it did no good."

"Momma, what are you talking about? When did you see me? Where was I?"

At this point she started to laugh, and I knew this was my mother being her usual prankish self.

"Oh baby, I was on the streetcar, there was no way you could see me. Edna even told me to open the window and stick my arm out, which I did, but you and Bone were busy talking. You had just come down the hill and were turning onto Fifth Avenue to enter the residence. Stan, the conductor, even slowed down a little, but of course he couldn't stop."

Edna was one of my mother's Tuesday friends. Each day domestics all over the city took the same trolley or streetcar to go to and from whatever house they were cleaning that day. After a while, many of them struck up friendships as they rode back and forth from their day's work. I had never met Edna but knew about her from my mother's conversation.

"I'll tell you what, Momma. Next Tuesday I'll make sure that I'm on the corner at 3:45 p.m. and I'll watch for the 76 Hamilton trolley so I can wave to you." We ended the conversation with her telling me to study hard and take care of myself.

That next Tuesday, the four of us were waiting eagerly for my mother's trolley, and when it came, we all waved, with Bone adding a piercing whistle.

"Hey Flur," said Bone. "If you caught the lights just right, you could run across Fifth Avenue, jump on the trolley, and give your mom a hug! Wouldn't that be something?"

"Don't be crazy," I retorted. "I'd probably fall and break my leg, or the light would change or something. I'm not running across Fifth Avenue! Especially at this time of day, when traffic is starting to build up, and it's not even a real streetcar stop!"

Every Tuesday that semester we did the same thing. Instead of staying inside and using the tunnel that connected the hospital to the nurses' residence, we would go out the side door of the hospital and walk down the hill toward the front entrance of school facing active Fifth Avenue. This was one of the busiest streets in the Oakland district of Pittsburgh, as it ran near four different hospitals and was also in close proximity to the University of Pittsburgh. Every week, Bone and I had some form of this same conversation. One of her ideas was to time the lights so maybe I could be on the other side of the street and wait for the trolley to come. If it had to stop for a light, I would be ready and waiting and could just jump on the trolley and see my mother that way. That sounded better to me, except I wouldn't be able to see if my mother was on the trolley until I actually got on.

Bone had an immediate solution: "We could signal you when we see her hand sticking out the window so you'd know this was the right trolley."

I told her I would think about it.

One Tuesday late in the semester, we watched as my mother's trolley rock slowly down Fifth Avenue. I could see her light brown hand sticking out the window ready to wave. Bone, always attentive, could see that the trolley was going to have to come to a full stop for a red light.

She started pounding me on the back, saying, "Get ready, Flur. You can make it today!"

"Bone, stop it! I'm not running across this busy street. I'll just wave as I always do." But she continued her pummeling and even offered to run with me.

It was only gradually that I became aware of a few things. First, Bone was no longer shouting in my ear or pounding on my back. Next, I realized that the starched white apron of my uniform was billowing out from my blue dress like the Flying Nun and my nurse's cap was bouncing up and down on my head. It wasn't until I felt the trolley tracks under my feet that I realized "Oh my God, I'm running!"

Many things crossed my mind as I ran: *Don't catch your foot in the tracks and break your ankle. Don't lose your cap because laundry hasn't been delivered this week and you don't have a clean one! Don't look at the light because you can't turn around and go back. What will I do if the conductor won't open the door? What if I get on the trolley and have to ride to the next stop?*

Too late. I was crossing in front of the trolley, and as I rounded the side the doors flew open! Up the steps I clambered, and spied my mother immediately. The look on her face was a mixture of astonishment, pride, and love. Leaning over a woman who I assumed was Edna, I gave my mother a kiss on the cheek.

"Hi Momma. I love you," I said. "I gotta go!"

The conductor said kindly from the front of the trolley, "You better hug her too 'cause it looks like we're gonna miss our next light!"

Most of the people who were sitting near my mother seemed fine with the delay, and some didn't seem to realize what was going on. Only one rider grumbled something about making extra stops.

Giving my mother a quick hug, Edna a quick wave,

and a breathless "Thank you," to the conductor, I jumped off the trolley, and since the light was still green for me, ran back across Fifth Avenue with a huge grin on my face.

My friends were clapping, Bone was whistling, and a few other students on their way into the residence stopped to see what was happening. I got to the other side and turned to give my mother one last wave. The other residents went inside, but the four of us stayed and waved at the trolley long after anyone on it could possibly see us.

Nancy McKeever

Donald

I watched as he sidled slowly toward me down the long hallway leading to the Diagnostic and Evaluation Center that was housed on the first floor of the Western Psychiatric Institute and Clinic in Pittsburgh.

My first experience in this prestigious hospital had been almost ten years earlier, when I was a student nurse doing a clinical rotation. After initially working on the inpatient units and with additional training, I now worked as a nurse clinician, the first evaluator of any patient who presented to the clinic. As a graduate RN, I had been taught to first note the patient's general appearance, behavior, and motor activity. What did I see before me now? A Black male, sixteen to eighteen years old. He was very thin and at that awkward stage where his body was a cluster of sharp angles, like a poorly drawn stick figure. It was as if someone had taken a bunch of wire hangers and stuffed them into a large sack. He was dressed sloppily in a shirt, pants, and jacket, all obviously too big for him. Even the belt holding up his sagging pants was tied in a messy knot. I found out later that the clothing belonged to his older brother. A Pittsburgh Pirates baseball cap was pulled low over his face. Walking closely alongside one wall, he looked over his shoulder as if he were checking to see if anyone was behind him. Fully absorbed in watching him, I thought, this already seems pretty straightforward. As an evaluating clinician, I was expected to gather a detailed and comprehensive history, but I was not an MD and legally could not diagnose patients. I could only document my "impression" of what I thought the diagnosis might be. I ticked off the symptoms I had noted thus far: late teens, disheveled, anxious, hypervigilant, and obviously paranoid. Impression: Paranoid Schizophrenia, first break.

"May I help you?" I asked, once he finally reached the desk.

Without looking directly at me, he said in a soft voice, "I wanna see a doctor."

I introduced myself and gently explained the evaluation process, letting him know that he first needed to speak with me and then would be seen by the physician. With some gentle but firm encouragement, he reluctantly agreed to talk with me after making sure that our conversation would not be overheard by others. I pointed out the individual private interview rooms to show him where our conversation would occur. He entered the interview room and settled uneasily in the indicated chair. Remembering one of the first rules of my training, I made sure that I was seated closest to the door in case I had to make a hasty exit. He told me his name was Donald.

"Do I hafta tell you my last name?" he asked as I probed to get basic demographic information.

"Not immediately, Donald, but at some point I will need your full name, address, date of birth, and parents' names."

Still not looking directly at me, but more over my right shoulder, he replied nervously, "Momma is dead and Daddy been in prison a long time. I been with my brother, and we been stayin' with different ones of his friends."

"And your brother, where is he now? You didn't want him with you tonight?"

Silence. Then he abruptly stood up as if to leave. I knew I needed to more firmly take charge of the situation. "Donald, sit down. You came here tonight because you wanted help. Let us help you. Are you afraid? Is someone after you?"

At this point, he collapsed into the chair, put his head face down on the desk, and pulled the huge coat over him as if to block out my voice, maybe other voices that only he heard or maybe the entire world. And then he began to cry. Huge body-wracking sobs like a young child. I let him cry until he finally raised his head, his face covered in tears and nasal mucous, looked directly at me for the first time, and said in one long breath: "He made me help them kill him. I didn't want to but what could I do? He and his friends stabbed him over and over. We cut up the body and put it in bags and threw them in the river! Somebody must have told though, 'cause in a few days the police came and we ran but they shot my brother Ronnie. I think he's dead. I'm not sure. We was stayin' at Gerald's house but he said I couldn't stay there no more because the police would be lookin' for me. So I been in the street. Nowhere to go, stealin' food, no sleep, and I'm tired, Miss Nancy. I'm tired."

For a few minutes, we just stared at each other. He, seemingly relieved. I was speechless. Was he delusional? Playing a game or telling me the truth? Sadly, my gut told me he was indeed telling the truth. Of course, he was paranoid and yes, people were after him and for good reason. He sat slumped in the chair, his body appearing shrunken like a deflated balloon. It was as if his confession had released all the tension he had been holding in for who knows how long and he could finally let go.

I found myself wondering why I was feeling so sorry for a confessed murderer. "Donald, do you realize this is a psychiatric hospital? I'm wondering why you came here. Are you saying you're mentally ill and that's why you helped your brother?"

"No, Miss Nancy. I want to give myself up, but I told you they shot Ronnie! I don't want them to shoot me too, so I thought if the doctor would talk to them and they would take me in but not just kill me!"

"So you want to talk to the doctor and have the police come here to pick you up. Is that right?"

"Yeah, that's what I want."

"Okay, Donald. I have to leave the room to call the doctor, tell him what you've told me, and he'll come down to talk to you. We'll proceed from there."

"Can't you call him from here?" He asked, pointing at the phone on the wall beside me. He was still paranoid, but rightly so and very observant from living a life where you had to be vigilant at all times in order to survive.

"You're right, Donald. I can call from here."

I was glad that Dr. Tom was on that night. A tall, boyish-looking man with curly brown hair and brown-rimmed glasses, you never saw him without a friendly smile or his pipe and tobacco stuffed in his left shirt pocket. Fortunately, all the residents were easy to work with, but Tom was one of my favorites and he would handle this as well as anyone could. I reached Tom in the residents' on-call room.

"Hi Tom, this is Nancy."

"Aw, Nance, I was just getting comfortable. This better be good!"

"Tom, I'm sitting with a seventeen-year-old Black male who has confessed to being forced by his older brother to help kill a man."

"Holy shit!" Tom said.

"They killed him, dismembered him, put the body parts in plastic bags, and threw them in the river. The police shot his brother, and we don't know if the brother is dead or alive. Donald has been running and hiding for weeks and wants our help in surrendering to the police. He's afraid he will be shot also."

"Holy shit!" Tom repeated. "Is he delusional or do you believe him?"

"I believe him, Tom. Get down here, please!"

As we waited for Tom, I reassured Donald that Tom would be helpful and kind and encouraged him to tell his story truthfully.

The interview with Tom went longer than most as he teased out the full details of the alleged crime. It gave me more time to process what had happened. As a Black woman raised in a poor neighborhood much like Donald's, I thought I had some idea of what his life had been like up until now, fighting the daily challenges of racism and poverty. I had lived such a life but was fortunate to have had a strong mother who always gave us hope. Gave us hope and helped us accomplish our goals with her unwavering support and optimism. I think the thought of no mother to guide him in this way made it seem even sadder to me. When Tom exited the room, he was shaking his head.

"He hasn't had a break all his life, and I feel badly for him, but we have to call the police. If we have to walk him all the way to the police car for him to feel safe, we will."

"You call the police and I'll get him something to eat." I sat quietly with Donald while he quickly ate the equivalent of two in-patient dinner trays.

"You're really brave, Donald, and I'm so sorry about all of this."

His only response was a resigned shrug of his shoulders. The police arrived fairly quickly and spoke with Tom in the area outside the evaluation center. When the conversation ended, Tom approached me first.

"Did you tell Donald we would walk him to the car?"

"No, I didn't, but it's okay, right?"

"They've asked that we not accompany him," he said. The tone of his voice let me know that I was not the only one feeling badly about this seventeen-year-old whose life before and after this night was unimaginable to both of us.

Together, Tom and I accompanied Donald to where the two policemen were waiting for him.

"We have to handcuff you, Donald," said one of the officers.

He extended his arms, and they quickly applied the cuffs to his skinny wrists. Donald turned to Tom and me and murmured "Thank you." He turned away and stared straight ahead, toward the same direction where he had entered.

Tom and I watched as Donald, still staring straight ahead, a policeman on each side, made his way down the long hallway, his handcuffed hands holding onto the huge knotted belt still precariously holding up his too large pants.

Donald never looked back, but all these years later I still do.

Nancy McKeever

Full Circle

It had been twenty-seven years since I last worked on Brotman Hospital's psychiatric unit, known as Pavilion 6 or P6, but I was now back in this same building where I started in 1977 when I first arrived in Los Angeles. It was almost like coming home, back to my first California work family.

I had come back to the old building to say goodbye to Nikki Stone, who was retiring; she was one of the few old staff who had remained. "Would you key me to P6, please?" I asked the security guard at the front desk, balancing my fruit pizza as I stuffed my keys and beeper into my lab coat pocket.

"You must be going to the party. I thought I had a taste of everything up there, but it looks like I missed something," he said, smiling, as he held up two neatly wrapped paper plates piled high with food. "I might have to make another trip!"

"Feel free to come and get another taste of dessert," I laughed.

Taking the specially keyed elevator to the sixth floor, I stepped off quickly, waved at Peggy, still the unit secretary, sitting at the front desk, and entered the already crowded nurses' station. I was immediately engulfed in the kind of party that only a group of nurses can give. The charting tables were pushed flush against the walls, the longest of the tables piled high with an array of food reflecting the diversity of the staff. I added my fruit pizza to the already packed smaller dessert table and noted that next to it was a small patient nightstand stocked with paper plates and aluminum foil for those guests who could not linger. Nurses can be so inventive and organized at times. In the middle of this celebration stood Nikki Stone, RN—the revered guest of honor. Nikki, who was one of the people who taught me to "trust my gut" and loosen my grip on a long-held practice. As a nurse manager, I had always thought it best for patients and staff that I hire only those applicants who had a minimum of two years' experience in acute in-patient psychiatry. I believed it was important to have staff who could quickly and accurately interpret both the verbal and nonverbal communications of patients, who could read the tone of the unit as soon as they stepped off the elevator, and who had the tools and strength to do a "takedown"—to de-escalate a possibly explosive situation. I believed these skills took time to learn.

As I made my way toward Nikki, I smiled, remembering her interview twenty-eight years ago in 1983, an interview I granted only because HR thought she seemed "so nice."

"I know you won't hire her as she is older and has absolutely no experience, but we can at least give her the experience of a good interview. Maybe you can think of some hospital that does hire inexperienced RNs," said Irma from HR.

"I'd be happy to interview her, Irma, and wish I could refer her to a psychiatric unit that was hiring new grads but I know Cedars, Saint John's, and NPI at UCLA aren't. I'll advise her as best I can."

Nikki arrived ten minutes before her scheduled appointment time. Peggy, our unit secretary even then, called me in my office, saying, "Your new applicant is here. She said she knows she's early and realizes she'll have to wait."

"No, bring her back. I'm ready."

"Thank you for seeing me early," Nikki said politely as she was shown into my office.

She was my height, about five-foot-seven, slim, and dressed neatly in a simple white blouse and plain blue skirt. She wore what my mother would have called sensible shoes, the kind that would allow you to walk around a unit for eight hours with no problem. Her dark hair ended slightly below her ears with just a ruffle of gray starting to peek through on the sides, framing a kind-looking face. Her only jewelry was small hoop earrings and a simple wristwatch. Although she stood ramrod straight, as if anchored by a steel spine, there was also an air of gentleness about her. She sat down, and in soft, matter-of fact tones told me about herself. How she had first been in nursing school at a time when marriage was not allowed. How she left school, chose marriage, and had one son who suffered from a mental disorder. How after her marriage ended in divorce, she returned to nursing school in her fifties. Now a graduate RN, she needed a job. We frankly discussed my "two years of experience" rule, but even as we talked, I knew I was going to hire this woman. Was it because she was "so nice," because I also had a child with a mental disorder, or because of her gentle strength? She had an obvious willingness and determination to learn and succeed. I felt a certainty in my gut that this would work. Much to HR's surprise, I hired Nikki. Both she and I were questioned separately, on different occasions, by staff who knew me and my rule well.

They asked me, "Who's going to teach her? What if we have to do a takedown? She's going to get hurt!"

"We will all teach her, and it will be incumbent on all of us to see that she does well. If she fails, it could mean that we failed her."

And so it began. Nikki did well from the very beginning. She was unafraid to admit she didn't know something and to ask questions, and this was key to her learning. Both staff and patients responded to her gentle, nonthreatening presence. Even the more disturbed patients seemed to know instinctively that this was someone they could trust and who would be gentle with them. She easily earned the admiration and respect of staff and physicians. By the time I left P6 for another position, Nikki had been fully accepted by staff, physicians, and, most importantly, patients. I had said goodbye to all staff when I left amid a party much like this one.

Now here I was, back with them, and it touched my heart to see them all, especially Nikki. We did get a few brief moments alone together where I was able to say goodbye, and I was surprised at the emotional impact it had on me. I felt very proud of Nikki and really, of the whole staff, who rose to the task of teaching this novice. I was like a proud momma who learns to watch their child and allows them to fully blossom into the person they were meant to be. I didn't discard my "two years of experience" rule but neither did I forget the importance of reexamining one's "rules" when the appropriate situation arose.

Nancy at Church

Stacey, Nancy Jean and Nancy,

Stacey, Nancy Jean, Heather, Nancy and Esther

MAKING A LIFE

True Confession

Dear Bill,

I have a confession to make. I've already admitted it to myself but I feel like I should admit it to the world, even though the person to whom it is directed is now deceased. I am referring to you, my husband, William Marcus McKeever, or Jeep, as your friends liked to call you, and the father of my children.

Here it is: my confession.

I knew I never should have married you, although I truly liked you a lot. I was always drawn to intelligent men, and you seemed extremely intelligent. Were you smart because you worked as a typesetter for the *Pittsburgh Post-Gazette* or did working for the *Post-Gazette* serve to enhance your intelligence? You were always great with words. You were the one who initiated me to more challenging crossword puzzles. My mother and sisters used to do simple crossword puzzles, but you encouraged me to try the ones in the Sunday paper...in ink. We had contests where we tried to beat each other completing them; I never won, and I didn't mind. Even losing was fun with you. You also introduced me to reading mystery novels. I started with Agatha Christie, then Nero Wolfe, on to John MacDonald, and now I'm into the Canadian writer

Louise Penny.

    I met you on New Year's Eve. I was out with Jackie (my sister-in-law) because her husband (my brother) did not want to go out. We went to a bar where Jackie's father was part owner. You were the first of many who bought us a drink. It was a fun night, and we felt quite safe since Jackie was well-known. I thought you were nice—the strong, silent type. Some of the guys there were a little loud and silly, but you seemed content to stand back and let them act as they chose. Somehow, I felt you were being protective in some way even though nothing was said. When we made a move to leave, you were still at the bar and encouraged us to stay, but I was not really interested and made some flippant remark as we left. I was very surprised when Jackie called me the next day to tell me that you had called her and asked for my number, and she had given it to you!

    "He's a nice guy," she kept saying. And then you called, we talked, and very soon we were dating. As I said, you were a nice guy. In thinking about it, I came up with this explanation. That was the summer when many of my friends were getting married. I probably went to six weddings and was a bridesmaid in four of them. It seemed like everybody was getting married, and I think I just wanted to be married too. Not a valid reason of course, but I think at the time it was easy to convince myself that I was in love. It was a lovely wedding. My Aunt Elizabeth, always the bargain hunter, took me to a secondhand bridal shop where gowns had been worn, cleaned, and then returned. I truly loved the gown we chose. It had a long train with delicate, intricate stitching. I don't remember how much it cost, but it was more than reasonable. When I walked down the aisle, it flowed behind me like a beautiful silken river.

We settled into a great two-bedroom apartment, a rental owned by my supervisor. I remember the rent was seventy-five dollars a month, a bargain at the time. We had three good years, maybe four. We were happy; Stacey was born, and you seemed glad to be a father and seemed so proud of her. When you took her to the bar when she was two, I thought you were just a proud father. But the bar trips with her increased, then the bar trips without her started. I began to worry about your job. Drunk almost every night, I knew you needed to be able to focus at your work as a typesetter, but how could you? You got angry when I tried to discuss this. Then came the day when your paycheck was much less than it should have been. It took a while for you to admit that you had been demoted. Just as it took the landlord (remember, my supervisor) a while to let me know that the rent had not been paid for two months! I was shocked and embarrassed. I can't remember where we got the money, but we did, and from then on when I cashed my check, I paid the rent. For a while, things seemed better, but they were not. By the time Nancy Jean was born five years later (why did I allow myself to get pregnant again?), you were spending most of your off time at the bar. By this time, you had pawned my wedding ring, emptied Stacey's piggy bank, threatened me with a gun (you thought I was having an affair with our fourteen-year-old paper boy), and been demoted to janitor at the newspaper. After the gun incident, I knew I had to get out, but how? I was working nights so that you could work days. I couldn't leave the girls at home by themselves. What could I do? It was then that my best friend Esther came to the rescue. She suggested that we live together. She offered to stay with our daughters at night. She promised me one year to get my schedule arranged. It was an unexpected godsend.

I planned the move in secret and left one day while you were at work. I was a bundle of nerves, thinking that any minute you were going to come around the corner and catch me. The psych techs from work, always helpful, moved me without asking a single question and accepting that the only way I could pay them was with beer and a spaghetti dinner cooked by Esther. Settling in was difficult, as you quickly found out where we were by following Stacey home from school. This resulted in a few nights of our daughters crying inside our new home while you drunkenly cried outside. But we both knew that I was never coming back. You knew you could visit the children as much as you wanted, but you did not seem to want to visit very often, especially if I wasn't with them. Once we got settled, things went smoothly, with only one hiccup. You initially refused to pay child support and, in addition, quit one of your jobs, trying to avoid any responsibility. You were ordered to pay seventy-five dollars a month for child support. You did pay for one or two months, but then stopped. At that time, no effort was made to track down delinquent fathers, so you were able to get away with it. There were a few times when you came to take Nancy Jean and Stacey out, and you left twenty or thirty dollars on the table. Certainly nothing I could count on.

When I told you about my plan to move to Los Angeles, you promised to come and visit, but that never happened. I think maybe it was easier for you if we were no longer in Pittsburgh. Was it? Our communication was sporadic, although our daughters were encouraged to keep in touch with you. You slowly became more impaired, resulting in various job changes at the paper, always to a lower level assignment there. You were soon diagnosed with pancreatic cancer caused by smoking and excessive alcohol consumption. You had a physician call me when they wanted to do surgery, as you said you didn't want to do it without my permission. I guess you just wanted me to know. The physician told me at that time that he did not expect you to live for very long. I asked him to call me when he thought I should send our daughters to say goodbye to you. He promised that he would. Some months after this discussion, he did indeed call to tell me it was time. I thanked him profusely, and very soon afterward sent our daughters to Pittsburgh to stay with my mom and visit you. They visited and came back with tales of how you were so thin that you wore your wristwatch on the upper part of your arm. They seemed to enjoy the time they spent with you, but I wondered if I'd done the right thing by letting them see you like that.

You died one month later.

I'm sorry for any part I played in this very sad story, but I hope you realize that I really did what I thought was the best at the time. I hope you're in a better place now.

Sincerely,

Nancy

From Friend to Family

It happened several nights a week. After all my other classmates had returned to the nurses' residence following their 3 p.m. to 11:30 p.m. shift, our colleague Sue Elek would storm off the elevator ranting, "That Jacox! She's driving me crazy. I can't do anything right!" Jacox was the last name of the charge nurse on the unit where we did our three-month psychiatric rotation. She and Elek had an obvious personality conflict. Although we teased Elek about her problems with this particular nurse, I also listened to her with some trepidation, because Flurry (my maiden name) followed Elek in the rotation, and I would soon be working with "that Jacox." Elek finished her rotation, and I was soon on the psychiatric unit with Esther Jacox as my charge nurse.

Esther was petite and white, with piercing brown eyes and a no-nonsense demeanor. She took her duties as charge nurse very seriously and could be seen scurrying down the long halls of the unit, short legs pumping, intent on giving the best possible care to her patients. She also had a dry sense of humor, which I appreciated from the very beginning. We managed to work together easily and quickly became friends. We remained friends through each of us dating, my marriage, the birth of my two daughters, and the failure of my marriage.

In 1972, after eight years of marriage and with two daughters aged two and seven, I began making plans to leave my alcoholic husband. Confident that our lives would be better without him, my biggest concern was childcare. With two young children, how could I continue to work the higher-paying night shift and still adequately care for them? Esther, now my best friend, generously offered to share a house with us. With Esther working days and me working nights, I knew my daughters would be well supervised at all times. Despite misgivings expressed by others, including "two women in one kitchen will never work," we made the decision to share a home. My daughters were ecstatic as they were already very close to Esther, because we had already been friends for eleven years. She had spent a great deal of time with my daughters, both with and without me. Before the days of mandatory seat belts, I remember Stacey, my older daughter, standing on the back seat of the car playing with Esther's hair as she drove her to some special outing. Esther had very fine hair, especially compared to Stacey's, and Stacey liked to refer to Esther's hair as "strings," and she'd amuse herself by fiddling with Esther's "strings" as they traveled together.

After some discussion, Esther and I agreed to a one-year commitment of living together, thinking that after a year, I could manage to be transferred to the day shift and could make other appropriate childcare arrangements. And so it was done. Esther, Stacey, Nancy Jean, and I moved into a carriage house on the outskirts of Highland Park in Pittsburgh. After an initial rough adjustment period, with their father coming, often in a crying, drunken state, to our front door, demanding that we return home and my needing to calm my daughters, who were concerned about Daddy being all alone, we settled into a very satisfying routine. Agreement on a household budget was quickly reached. Esther seemed to enjoy her role as godmother to two little girls, and I was grateful for the financial and emotional support. The year passed quickly and easily. But plans changed, as plans often do, and before the end of that year, Esther was pregnant.

Being a strong-willed woman from a small lily-white town outside of Erie, Pennsylvania, called Hawthorn, Esther had to tell her straitlaced mother and ten siblings that not only was she unmarried and pregnant, but the father was a Black man. This was totally unacceptable to them, and after weeks of berating her by phone, her entire family withdrew from her.

During Esther's pregnancy, we discussed the idea of continuing our living arrangement for another year, as there were now three children to consider. Both of us agreed that this would continue to benefit all five of us. My daughters were delighted that Esther would continue to live with us and started making plans for the arrival of what we decided would be a brother. We named him Jeffrey. I can still see two-year-old Nancy Jean squatting down, as only a two-year-old can do, with her mouth close to Esther's abdomen, shouting, "Hi, Jeffrey! Can you hear me?"

While waiting for the baby to be born and having no support from her own family, Esther became closer to my mother and often spent time with her. When her baby girl, Heather, was born, she was given the middle name of Sue to honor my mother. The girls decided it was better to have a sister after all. Esther did not see her family, nor did they see her or their granddaughter until Heather was one year old.

As an infant, Heather was closely monitored by her two "sisters," especially eight-year-old Stacey, who, each time Heather would become fussy and cry, would proclaim loudly in an imperious voice, "Esther, your baby is crying!"

As time passed and Heather learned to talk, she called me "Mommie," as my daughters did, and called Esther by her name as my daughters did, although she knew that Esther was her mother. It was as if my name was Mommie just as hers was Heather. Some jealousy on Nancy Jean's part was evident. She reminded Heather that I was NOT her real mother and that Nancy Jean's grandmother was NOT Heather's real grandmother. This only lasted a short time, and Heather soon began calling me Godmother. Today, at the age of 42, she calls me Godmother Girl.

The years passed, and we continued on: three girls and two mothers. There was no discussion of changing. We did everything as a family.

In 1977, after a vacation in Los Angeles to visit my two sisters, I decided to relocate. Unsure at first, Esther eventually decided to move also, and so our family remained intact.

With three active children, there were many extracurricular activities to attend once we settled in L.A. Stacey was in the band, Nancy Jean had dance programs, and Heather had synchronized swimming competitions. There was never a question about the family supporting all events, and we attended these events as a family group.

There was always music in the house, for we all loved all kinds of music and the three girls loved to sing and dance. Our life as a family continued against the background of classical music along with Herb Alpert, Blood, Sweat & Tears, Roberta Flack, Carole King, Prince, Journey, The Eagles, Elton John, Michael Jackson, and so many others. The family joke was that Esther never knew the correct lyrics to a song, and the girls would go into gales of laughter when she would sing along and repeat the verses incorrectly.

Their preteen and teenage years, with the usual teenage complications, were manageable, and we continued to support each other through difficult events such as Nancy Jean's Tourette's syndrome and more mundane problems such as preventing the two younger ones from attempting to spy on Stacey and her first real boyfriend. The house rule was no boys in the house unless Esther or I was home. Many days we turned on to Gibson Street off Robertson Boulevard after working the day shift and saw our front yard dotted with boys of various ages, colors, shapes, and sizes, looking like sheep grazing in the countryside. Our house was lively, musical, and fun, and the gathering place of the neighborhood.

In 1991, Heather broached the subject of wanting to find an apartment for her and Esther, Nancy Jean wanted to move in with a friend, and Stacey, ever her mother's daughter, wanted to remain for a short while with me. The decision was made as all decisions had been made over our long time of living together, with open discussion and easy acceptance of each other's wishes.

We had grown together as a family. Esther and I had gone from a friendship, to a one-year commitment of sharing a home together, and finally to eighteen years of raising three daughters together. It was not always an idyllic situation, but we all felt connected, cared for, and loved. Esther has now been a part of my life for longer than she has not been a part of it. "That Jacox" has been my friend for fifty-four years. Fifty-four years and counting.

Nancy McKeever

Swimming Lessons

"Let's go, lady," she said laughingly, the deep dimple showing in her left cheek just like her father's. After riding three buses to get to my house at 8:30 in the morning, my youngest daughter was eager to get to the Santa Monica Aquatic Center to help me attempt to improve my poor swimming skills. I had made a vow to learn how to swim, but after eight thirty-minute group sessions, my "swimming" still consisted of an uncoordinated series of sudden stops and starts as I attempted to synchronize all the necessary movements. In my head, I had visions of gliding smoothly through the water like all those other swimmers I had envied through the years, the water glistening on my skin, the sun shining brightly above, and me slipping through the water as smoothly as a rainbow trout. In reality, I could only accomplish a few weak strokes before I forgot to kick or forgot to stroke or forgot to breathe! I needed practice, but I also needed the assistance of someone encouraging, supportive, and most importantly...patient.

Because of her own life experiences in practicing patience and her strong "willing to help" attitude, I accepted my daughter's spontaneous offer to practice with me. This generosity of spirit, an acute awareness of other's needs, and compassion for others has always framed her every interaction for as long as I can remember. She has had many personal struggles in her life and come through very difficult situations with renewed strength and determination. Nancy Jean, and yes, we have the same name, was diagnosed with Tourette's syndrome at age nine. At the time she was diagnosed, I was separated from her father and had started sharing a household with my best friend Esther and her six-year-daughter. Stacey, Nancy Jean's sister, was fourteen. She was the first person to notice Nancy Jean's symptoms and correctly name them, but we all learned about Tourette's syndrome together.

Tourette's syndrome is an inherited neuropsychiatric disease characterized by involuntary vocal and muscular tics. The vocal tics can be words or sounds blurted out loudly and often include profanity. The muscular tics can include sudden movements of the arms, pelvis, legs, or feet. A person with Tourette's can suppress the tics for a while, but sooner or later they must be released. The tics are only absent during sleep. Stress aggravates the tics, and the stress of trying to suppress them only makes them erupt more violently.

Attending school definitely increased Nancy Jean's stress level, as very few people, including teachers, were aware of nor understood the symptoms of

Tourette's. Some teachers saw her behavior as voluntary and punished her by making her leave the room. They didn't understand that the tics could be suppressed for a while but would inevitably erupt. Although she had many friends, there were also those students who teased her. On the street, on a bus, or in a store, Nancy Jean would tic, sometimes saying the f-word, and those around us would react with shock and/or disgust. Our family, with no words exchanged between us, would close ranks around her so she felt protected. I would be blind with rage and want to rail against everyone who was so quick to judge what they did not understand. Nancy Jean, on the other hand, would sometimes approach these strangers and attempt to explain her situation to them. Sometimes this was successful and sometimes not. I felt guilty when I learned this was a genetic disease passed on to my child by me. A well-known neurologist who examined Nancy Jean also thought that because of the severity of her symptoms, her father must have carried the gene also. Stacey has said that she often felt overshadowed by Nancy Jean's illness, as her needs seemed to outweigh all others. This is undoubtedly true, but I have accepted the fact that as a parent, I did the best I could do at the time and we must now live with my decisions. Quick-witted, intelligent, and energetic, Nancy Jean made excellent grades in school, had many friends, and was especially interested in dance and choreography. At age fourteen, she was teaching adults at the Steven Peck Dance Studio in exchange for extra dance classes. This was the perfect setting for her, as the loud dance music muffled the sound of her tics. Upon the recommendation of her junior high school dance teacher and after a strenuous audition, she was accepted into the first class of the Los Angeles County High School for the Arts, which was housed on the campus of Cal State L.A. A promising future seemed to stretch ahead of her. Despite her difficulties with the symptoms of Tourette's, she was still making her way successfully in the world.

Initially, she did well in this school and seemed to enjoy herself, but that soon changed. Due to missing multiple classes and falling grades, which, unknown to me at the time, were the first symptoms of the need for psychiatric intervention, Nancy Jean was asked to leave this very special program. Disappointed, angry with myself, and feeling guilty, again, for being so involved with work that I hadn't noticed a change in her behavior and unsure of how to explain this change in personality, I quickly enrolled Nancy Jean in another L.A. high school. She successfully graduated from this school. After graduation, she tried working in various fast-food restaurants, but unfortunately her tics were too disruptive to customers and coworkers. Soon after this, Nancy

Jean experienced her first manic episode and then her first psychiatric hospitalization, at Cedars-Sinai Hospital. Her Tourette's, which had seemed fairly stable, was exacerbated by the addition of psychotropic medication, and it would be several years before those meds would be stabilized again. During the ensuing years, she would be in and out of hospitals: stable and then unstable psychiatrically, and eventually homeless after walking out of her fully furnished apartment as she became fearful of remaining there. She left Los Angeles, moved up north to stay with friends for a short while, and finally returned to L.A.

For the past three years, Nancy Jean has lived in and maintained her own apartment. Her Tourette's is stable although she still has multiple tics and continues to deal with negative reactions from others on a daily basis. She works part-time as an in-home caretaker for Esther, who now suffers from Parkinson's disease. Funny, quick-witted, and loving, she is compassionate with everyone with whom she comes in contact. She is very family-oriented and keeps in touch with aunts, uncles, and cousins, and can always be counted on to remember everyone's birthday, anniversary and any other important life event.

I think about Nancy Jean's challenges and triumphs as I watch her standing confidently in the pool, giving directions and shouting encouragement to me. I wonder about the source of her continued strength and perseverance. As her mother, I can only hope that she will continue to be strong, to face her struggles head-on, to enjoy each moment of her life as best she can, and to know that she is deeply admired and loved. She inspires me to try my hardest, to never give in or give up. So there she stands before me, arms outstretched and calling out to me, "You're badass! Come on! Just float to me. Don't worry, I won't let you fall." I take a deep breath, push off the side of the pool, and float into my amazing daughter's arms.

Nancy McKeever

Momma Was Right

Her weekly ironing completed and neatly put away, my mother dried her sweaty face with the hem of her faded cotton apron and moved purposefully from the kitchen to the living room. She settled comfortably in her favorite chair and stated wearily, as she had many times before, "Every woman should have a wife!"

I wonder what her reaction would be today if she knew that I now both have and am a wife? Unquestionably, my mother was not talking about the role of a wife in a lesbian relationship.

I think she would understand that after multiple failed relationships with men, one failed marriage to a man, and, at the age of forty-nine a disquieting affair with my female supervisor, I was thoroughly confused. The impact of being sexually attracted to a woman sent me dashing to a therapist like a sprinter headed for the tape at the finish line. I was anxious, shocked, and also a little titillated by the direction in which my life was headed. What was going on with me? What had I been thinking all my life? Who was I? Was I "just a lonely heterosexual woman," as my very religious friend Esther said when I shared this information with the family we had created as friends? The impact of this declaration to this group only led to more questions that I was unable to answer. Was I bisexual, a lesbian, or maybe someone who couldn't or shouldn't be labelled?

So many questions with no simple answers. While the female relationship didn't last either, the therapy thankfully did. A process where I allowed myself to be peeled like an onion, layer by painstaking layer, discovering things about myself that surprised, displeased, and, at times, gratified me.

Examining those failed relationships helped me to realize that I had never learned to put myself first. I was a very cautious and conventional person. A people pleaser who had difficulty identifying, let alone expressing, my needs. Unable to articulate my wants but expecting them to be fulfilled. One big life lesson: "If you can't identify what you want, you can't ask for it, and if you can't ask for it, you'll probably never get it."

What did I do with this newfound knowledge? I tried to live life more fully and less cautiously. I spent time identifying what I wanted, like finally planning that trip to Paris, and taking the necessary steps to make it happen. While not actively looking for a significant other of either sex, I continued working, socializing with family and friends, and waiting for the next chapter of my life to unfold.

At age sixty-three, I was approached by a colleague

who casually asked if I was interested in meeting a friend of a friend.

"I don't know her that well, but I think you two would like each other. You seem to enjoy doing some of the same things: Disney Hall, plays, ballet. She also likes to travel. It doesn't have to be any more than a friendship. You two could just meet for coffee or something. If you'd like, you could meet at our house, and Sheila and I could be the buffers."

Why not? I had nothing to lose.

For various reasons, the buffered coffee date never occurred, but phone numbers were exchanged, and Patty Antin and I finally spoke by phone. I don't recall much of the content of our first conversation, but I do remember that it lasted much longer than I expected. In keeping with my "take care of yourself" goal, I used the opportunity to exert my newly acquired assertiveness to deliver this message.

"I only want to spend time with someone sane. No drama allowed!"

"Great minds think alike." She laughed, and plans were made.

By the end of the conversation, coffee had morphed into dinner. I chose a familiar restaurant convenient to my home. She agreed, and the date was set.

First impression: A full head of silky-looking curly

white hair framed a pleasant, dimpled face. It was anchored by a smile so wide and warm and welcoming it was like looking into a pool of warm honey, and I wanted to dive right in. Love at first sight? No, but a sight that touched something inside me that said "more."

Even my familiar restaurant seemed different that night, somehow warmer and brighter and more festive. After a delightful dinner and interesting conversation, we parted pleasantly and in ten minutes I was home. Continuing my pledge to be less cautious and more trusting of my instincts, I called her home phone so there would be a message waiting when she arrived.

"Great evening, Patty. Hopefully, we'll do it again sometime."

We talked several times during that first week. Each conversation easy, effortless, and enjoyable. Gradually getting to know each other better and better while at the same time feeling as if we had known each other forever. We never stopped seeing each other after that very first Saturday, and I found myself looking forward to each subsequent encounter with the anticipatory excitement of a child at Christmas. Love in my sixties?

Whether it was age or not, we moved slowly into our deepening relationship, too slowly in the opinion of both her friends and mine. When I related to my friend Linda (twenty years my junior, and "out" most of her life) that I would come home from work several days a week and find a bud vase of garden flowers waiting for me on my porch, she asked indignantly, "Well, what are you waiting for? It's obvious she likes you and you like her. Time to move in together!"

It took us two years to make the decision. In that two-year period, we managed to fit in that long-planned trip to Paris. Eager, but also somewhat anxious, we joined households, making sure that I retained all my beloved antiques and other favorite items while insuring that her belongings were not displaced. Everything fit perfectly, as if by magic, and even my furniture seemed to welcome the move. My corner hutch, which had stood tall and stately in my spacious Spanish-style Bedford Street dining room looked even better in our new home. The old hutch expanded into its new space, flexed its dark pine sides, and heaved a sigh of pleasure as it appeared to spread out and reveal its full beauty. My ladies writing desk pranced delicately into an alcove in the guest bedroom, and the Chinese cabinet with the removable doors also had the perfect place waiting for it.

Everything came together easily, and while there were occasional moments of disagreement, there was and still is always the willingness to talk, to try to understand the other's perspective, to compromise and to work at protecting what we both feel is special, is good, is forever.

So, thirteen years later, I'm finally clear as to who I am, and it does not include a label of any kind. I am Nancy. A woman who loves and is loved by another woman. We are both loving, generous of spirit, endlessly supportive, and fiercely protective of our life together. With all my quirks, idiosyncrasies, and flaws, she loves me and I her.

Our one regret is that Patty never met my mother face to face. In our weekly phone conversations, my mother would always inquire about my "roommate Patty" in the same way she would ask about my openly gay brother's "roommate," but we never addressed the issue directly. Did she know the true nature of our relationship? I'll never know. But I continue to chat with her sometimes in my head and remind her that, as far as Patty and I are concerned, she was absolutely right.

Every woman needs a wife.

Nancy and Patty

No Fool, No Fun

Mimsi, Judy, Susie, Shirley (Snip) and Nancy

GOING HOME

No Regrets

She's told me the story many times, and I picture it in my head like a scene from a black-and-white movie. Two young girls, eleven and thirteen years old, are begrudgingly bringing the family's four cows home from the pasture. One sister (Susie, my mother) is taller though younger than the other. She is slim, caramel-colored, and quieter than her older sister but just as unhappy about the cow situation. The shorter, older sister, Clara. is not quite as thin as her sibling, has a slightly darker skin tone, and is much more vocal about the situation. "Why is it never "Sarah and Emma, please go get the cows? And what about the boys? They could do it on their way home with Pop. But no, it's always Clara and Susie. Momma says the same thing every time: 'It's time, girls. I shouldn't have to remind you all every day.' Well, maybe that means we shouldn't be doing it every day!"

They continued down the dusty road toward home. Barefoot, kicking up small puffs of dust as they walked, sometimes stepping onto an unnoticed cow patty.

"Damn!" Clara would exclaim. "Now it's cow shit. I hate this!"

"Why was it always you and Aunt Clara, Momma? Why didn't you take turns?"

"I don't know, baby. That's just the way it was, and yes, we fussed about it, but we still did it."

That was just one of the stories from her childhood that my mother told me. She did relate, briefly, about her mother dying after a surgical procedure,. She couldn't name the surgery and could only say her mother never came home from the hospital. It seemed to me that there was still a tinge of sadness in her voice when she mentioned her mother's death. She was only twelve. I know that perhaps a year after her mother's death, she and her three sisters were sent to live with their father's sister, also named Sue. My mother describes her as a cold, cranky person who used to berate her for her voracious reading habit.

I think of these snippets of my mother's life, gathered during my yearly visits to her in Pittsburgh. It was a quiet, peaceful, rejuvenating time for me. A time when I could be with Susie, as I sometimes called her, and once again soak up all that healing energy that she seemed to exude so easily. I would tell her all my concerns, frustrations, and mistakes. Not that she had any answers for me, and only infrequently a suggestion or two, but somehow in the sharing and telling of these big and small concerns with Momma/Susie, many things fell into place, and what had seemed a big problem now felt manageable.

I regret that I didn't use my time with her differently.

Instead of allowing myself to wallow in the warmth of her seemingly endless patience and love, I wish I had asked for more details of her life. I know that my parents married young. She was eighteen and he seventeen. I know that my mother dearly loved her mother-in-law and felt that she and her children were loved in return. She would describe in great detail how after taking my oldest brother and sister to visit with their Grandma, Mrs. Flurry would climb up on the trolley car with my mother and the toddlers.

"You just hold on a minute," she would tell the conductor.

"Let me get my grandbabies settled and I'll be gettin' back off."

The whole trolley would have to wait while Grandma took good care of her "grandbabies," as she called them. I wish I had known my father's mother. Would he have acted differently if she had been alive? Would he still have had two families if she had been around? How could he have explained this to her? Momma never mentioned his father, and I don't remember asking about him. Another missed opportunity. The only one of my grandparents that I ever met was my maternal grandfather. I'll never forget his visit. He was a tall, slender man; he looked at least six-foot-six to me. I remember that he came to visit when I was approximately twelve years old. We were so excited as Momma asked us to fix him breakfast and a "light" lunch. His breakfast consisted of bacon, eggs, potatoes, toast, and two cups of coffee and we were delighted when he ate it all. When my mother came home from work and we were chattering with excitement, she asked about his breakfast and lunch. When he described what he had eaten, she exclaimed, "But Pop, you don't like eggs."

His firm response: "I do now!" I will always remember that moment. The small but proud smile on my mother's face and the knowledge that we had done something to please both of them. The second memorable moment was his baking us a cake. No recipe, no measurements, just these two large hands quickly and easily making one of the best-tasting cakes I had ever had. When we told him how good the cake was, he responded, "I teached your Momma how to cook, you know; she cooks almost as good as me!" Again, her response was just that same small smile, which, to me, said "Look at them enjoying each other!"

We enjoyed our grandfather's only visit, and hopefully he enjoyed it too. We never saw him again.

Given her life, how did my mother move from herding cows and skipping over cow patties to quoting Shakespeare, memorizing and reciting in dialect various poems like "The Party" by Paul Laurence Dunbar? How did she know about the famous French painting

September Morn, a phrase she used to greet us with in the morning when she would enter our room and find us in varying states of undress? Did they have books on the farm, at Aunt Sue's, or did she have access to a library?

What was the inspiration for her wanting to be a French teacher? She threw out many common French phrases, but also some in Spanish.

Although I no longer sat on her ample lap, we talked for hours. She sat in her lounge chair, which gave her the opportunity to look out the large living room window at passers-by on the one-block-long Conemaugh Street or turn slightly to the right and have a perfect view of the TV when it was time for her soap operas. I would be positioned across the room lying on the sofa, lying so I could look directly into that beloved face. Smooth skin even in her nineties, dark hair with a halo of gray around her face, her same sweet smile showing the gap between her two front teeth that she passed on to all of her children.

I've been thinking of her a lot lately, more than usual. I'm sure it's because both my life and the world seem so out of control. Oh, for a chance to once more lie on the sofa across from her, empty my woes into her seemingly bottomless lap, and to feel that sense of relief when she would start the conversation, as she always did, with, "Well, baby, let's take one thing at a time."

Although she never framed it in this way, maybe our

conversation reminded me that compared to her life, my life was so much easier. I had the luxury of growing up in a different era than she, and I had many more opportunities. With the pillow of a good nursing education, which led to a well-paying job, I had the ability, even without a husband, to live well and adequately provide for my children. No cleaning other people's homes for a living, no need to miss a meal so my children could eat, no remaining tied to a husband with two families. I could live my life with less of the burden women like my mother carried when dealing with racism, misogyny, and poverty.

I think now of those moments, and though they are few, at least I have them. If I keep them in that special place where all our special memories go, I should have no regrets at all.

No Fool, No Fun

As young children, we lived under a cloud of poverty. Never enough money, clothes, or individual space. In spite of this, or maybe because of it, we learned to be very creative in order to have fun in the simplest ways, whether it was following after my brother Billy, dancing around the apartment while he used a towel to pretend he was playing a saxophone, or running from my brother Chuckie as he chased us with "Snodgras," an old fake fox boa with the head attached, causing us to run and scream with laughter. When we acted this way, my mother would smile, shake her head, and say, "No fool, no fun."

This became a familiar phrase in our household, and we used it often, usually to explain away some prank we had played on a sibling. As we grew older, the phrase was used less often, but we remained a family that loved to joke and play.

In the summer of 1987, we decided to have a Flurry family reunion in Pittsburgh, including my mother and father, their six children, and eight of their eleven grandchildren. At this time, my father was seventy-four and my mother seventy-three. My siblings ranged in age from forty to fifty-five, hardly children, but still ready for a good laugh at any opportunity.

Nancy McKeever

What started out as a Flurry reunion soon grew to include my mother's three sisters who also lived in Pittsburgh, and their children and grandchildren. This was great news for everyone as we were close to our aunts and cousins. Our Aunt Clara and her children were our favorites as when we were very young, my mother would go to work one day while Aunt Clara watched both sets of children (a total of eight). The next day, the roles would be reversed while Aunt Clara worked, and my mother watched the children. For a while, my older brother and sister called my parents Susie and Thurston just like my cousins, but my mother quickly put a stop to that. As adults, we sometimes jokingly but lovingly referred to them by their first names. Acceptable by this time as part of the unwritten "no fool, no fun" code.

Plans were made for me and Snip and Mimsi along with our children to fly into Pittsburgh from Los Angeles. Chuckie would arrive form Rochester, New York, and my cousins from Minnesota, Chicago, and New Jersey.

On Friday night as we prepared to drive to the airport to pick up my older daughter Stacey, who would be arriving in Pittsburgh from the University of California at Santa Cruz, Billy made an announcement with the family gathered.

"I wanted everyone to have a souvenir from this reunion. You know how some families have T-shirts or caps, common things like that? But since the Flurrys are so very special, I bought us something very special."

Reaching into a bag he was holding in his left hand, he pulled out three types of noses with black elastic bands attached.

"What are those?" said Judy. "Some kind of animal noses?"

We all looked at the noses—there were the pink and white noses of a rabbit with two big front teeth, the round black dog noses, and finally, pig noses with two little piggy nostrils.

"Indeed they are, Judith Ann," he said. Billy always called us by our first and middle names when he was trying to emphasize his big brother role. Either that or "man," and it didn't matter if you were male or female. "I have one for all of you and your children. I expect everyone to wear their chosen nose with pride because only a true Flurry can carry something like this off! We're going to start by wearing them to the airport tonight. Take your pick!"

"Something's wrong with that boy, Sue," said my father.

"Thurston, you know what I always say."

"No fool, no fun," we all said in unison.

Everyone laughed, but I thought about Stacey, and how private and unobtrusive she liked to be. I knew she would be embarrassed, at least initially.

"You will embarrass my daughter to death!"

"Nancy, your daughter has Flurry blood in her veins, and she'll do just fine. After all, she'll be walking with her favorite uncle," Billy said, smiling devilishly.

Little Nancy, as my youngest daughter was called at the time, said gleefully, "Stacey's gonna freak! I'll wear a nose! Uncle Billy and Ema (my daughter's nickname for me), you have to wear one too!"

"Okay, I guess I'm wearing a nose! She'll forgive me eventually."

By this time, everyone had joined the discussion, and the more we talked the funnier it became.

"I think I might have to go too," said Chuckie. C'mon, Snip and Judy, all the Flurrys can go. Billy and I will drive, and all you have to do is wear your nose!"

And that's what we did. Billy and Little Nancy and me in one car, and Chuckie, Snip, Mimsi, and Judy in another. Off to Pittsburgh International Airport we went.

When we arrived at the airport, but before entering, Billy laid down some ground rules.

"Look, man, we cannot go in there laughing and giggling. We have to act like we're a normal family just going to pick up a family member. We have enough time so we might even want to stop in a shop to get a Pittsburgh souvenir to remind you of this momentous occasion."

"Normal?" Mimsi snorted. "Stop and shop? Thurston's right, there is something wrong with you!"

"Miriam Louise, we will act like we do this every day. Like this is nothing out of the ordinary."

After a few false starts, with one or the other of us breaking into fits of laughter, we entered the airport. Chuckie and Snip, arm in arm, were in the lead, strolling casually through the busy airport. They were followed by Judy and Mimsi, who walked with their heads close together, whispering in a conspiratorial manner. Billy, Little Nancy, and I brought up the rear so Billy could "keep an eye on everyone."

That's when the real fun began. Some people tried to pretend they weren't really looking at us and peered furtively out of the corner of their eyes; some stared openly, their mouths agape, and others laughed outright. The most common reaction was a double take, where someone would glance up, then look away, suddenly realize what they thought they saw, and quickly try to catch another glimpse before we passed them by. We made our way to the appropriate gate. We would alert each other as unobtrusively as possible to any over-the-top reaction. For example, one woman tried to get her husband's attention as we passed, frantically tugging on his shirtsleeve. He was busy looking into a store window and she finally punched him soundly on the arm to get his attention, but by this time we had gone past where they were standing.

"With any luck, we'll catch those two on the way back!" said Billy.

We did stop at one store on the way, where Billy purchased a crossword puzzle magazine for my mother. He and I went into the store together while the other five stood outside peering into the window. The store clerk looked at the two of us, then at the group staring in the window, and in his amazement, managed to drop our change on the floor. He looked at the other patrons as if to say, *Do you see this?* We completed our purchase and walked calmly from the store.

"A true Flurry, Nancy Jean," my brother said as we exited the store.

There were similar reactions as we waited at the gate for Stacey. Everyone was trying to figure out what we were doing and why. Finally, passengers started to exit the plane and walk down the ramp to their waiting families. Soon we saw Stacey walking briskly down the ramp toward us. At least she started off briskly. As she approached, the closer she got to us, the slower she walked. You could tell by the quizzical look on her face that she was not sure of what she was seeing. Almost reaching the bottom of the ramp, she realized what was going on. She came to a complete stop, hesitated for a minute, did a quick about-face and headed back up the ramp and back onto the plane. At this point, we could no longer keep straight faces and we burst out laughing.

"Oh my goodness! My poor daughter will never get off that plane!"

"Nancy Jean, just be patient. She has to come back! They won't let her hide on the plane forever!"

In a few minutes, she reappeared. This time she walked slowly down the ramp with her head down.

She came directly to me.

"Mom, everyone is looking at all of you. You people are crazy!"

"Oh no, Stacey, they're not looking at us," said Billy, putting his arm around her shoulder. "They're looking at you because you're the only one that doesn't have a nose, but I have one for you right here."

With that, Billy took a nose out of his jacket pocket and handed it to Stacey. She looked at me and her sister and her aunts and uncles and finally gave a tentative smile.

"I guess if I want to get out of this airport and see my Grandma, I'd better wear this stupid thing."

With that, she put on her nose and with their Uncle Billy between them, my daughters led us back the way we had come and out of the airport. The return trip was just as eventful as the trip in, with us again enjoying the varied reactions of the people we passed. Even Stacey relaxed enough to enjoy the pure foolishness of it all.

When we returned to Judy's house, everyone wanted to know if we had actually worn the noses and then wanted a detailed description of everyone's reactions.

"There'll probably be a picture on the front page of the *Pittsburgh Post-Gazette*," said Judy sarcastically. "And all of you will be gone, leaving me here with Billy!»

"Hey, man, we'll be famous, the Fabulous Flurrys!" he said.

We all laughed.

We took many photos over those three days: individual ones and various groupings, some candid and some posed. One of my favorites was taken in my sister's backyard. It's a side view of the whole family, with Susie and Thurston sitting in front on two wooden folding chairs. Behind them, in no particular order, are their six adult children, each wearing their chosen Fabulous Flurry nose.

Try a Little Tenderness

It was an example of a high level of organization balanced against a pillow of subtle tenderness. A project planned and thoroughly thought out to gain the most possible efficacy and imparted with an unspoken element of warmth and delicacy. The task I'm referring to is my mother's weekly ironing. It was Tuesday and my mother's unchanging schedule was laundry on Monday and ironing on Tuesday. This was in the 1980s, and I was visiting Pittsburgh from Los Angeles, but it could have been thirty years earlier, as her actions and equipment were all so familiar to me. She still used an old wringer washer because she thought it "cleaned the clothes better." When her last wringer washer broke down, we had pleaded with her to get an electric washer, but she was adamant about what she wanted. It wasn't easy to find a wringer washer at that time, and I can't remember where we finally obtained one, but we did. She did consent to using an electric dryer, but that's as much as she would compromise.

On this Tuesday, all the necessary equipment was in place. The old iron with no jets for steam, just a flat metal surface to glide over the clothes; the ironing board, whose cover had worn out long ago, and was now neatly covered with an old tablecloth held securely in place by two large safety pins; and the sprinkling bottle, which was used since there was no steam, and which had at one time held some other liquid. After being thoroughly washed, an ice pick was used to punch holes into the top so that water could sprinkle out when needed, and it sat ready at the end of the ironing board on my mother's right side. On her left, toward the head of the ironing board but on the floor, sat the basket of already sprinkled clothes, each rolled into a ball waiting for the magic of ironing to occur.

The last accessory to complete the picture was the old Philco radio that sat on a little stand against the back kitchen wall. My mother always played the radio as she ironed and sang along with the old songs she loved. She preferred the older songs, so she listened to KDKA or maybe it was WJAS who played the older singers like Bing Crosby, Peggy Lee, and Frank Sinatra. One of her favorite songs was "Try a Little Tenderness."

"She may be weary; women do get weary wearing the same shabby dress. But when she's weary, try a little tenderness." It always made me a little sad hearing her sing this song. Not because of anything she said or did but because in my mind, I wondered if she was thinking about herself. After all, she had had a difficult life. Seven children and a husband who gave very little emotional or financial support for many years, although by this time he seemed happily settled at home with my mother. She seemed equally happy to have him there. It was evident in their daily interactions, in his occasional gift of a box of her favorite candy—chocolate-covered cherries—or when he stuffed a few bills into her apron pocket, saying, "I heard you telling Trick [Clara, who she talked to every day] that you saw a pair of shoes you liked in East Liberty. Go get them." They would go to the movies on Saturday night, and most Sundays he accompanied her to Saint Mark's AME church, leaving before the service was over but waiting patiently outside when she exited.

For her part, she cooked him three hot meals a day, even in the humid summers of Pittsburgh, and always made sure he had an unending supply of iced tea and his favorite Whitehouse ice cream.

But I also saw it in her weekly ironing of their clothes. My mother ironed everything. The usual shirts and blouses and tablecloths, but she also ironed dish towels, sheets, pillowcases, dresser scarves, my father's ever-present handkerchiefs, and even his boxer shorts. I often wondered why she ironed his shorts, but she took as much care with them as she did with his shirts. She would iron the shirts and hang them neatly from any available kitchen cabinet knob. The shirts marched around the kitchen walls stiff from the spray starch that she had finally deigned to use after years of using Argo starch, which came in a blue box and had to be mixed with water. His shorts, while not starched, were carefully ironed, then neatly folded and aligned so they looked like a men's store display. His handkerchiefs would be folded with the edges touching. If the handkerchief happened to be have his initial on it, she would make sure the T for Thurston was properly displayed. Sometimes, she would neatly fold back one corner. I'm not sure whether that was to make sure he could easily pick it up or just an extra little flourish on her part.

Many Tuesday afternoons I would be relaxing on the sofa in the living room and could still follow her movements from the sounds I heard in the kitchen. She would take an article of damp clothing from the basket and I would hear the sharp snap as she shook it open before placing it on the ironing board. She would check to make sure it was still damp enough and didn't require more sprinkling before she began. Once she started ironing, I could hear the occasional hiss of steam as the iron glided over the clothes or the creak of the ironing board as she applied enough pressure to get out every wrinkle. I heard the whoosh of the spray starch as she ironed my father's shirts and dresser scarves that carried with it a very distinct smell, which I can remember even today. It smelled clean and fresh. In a very short time, I could hear the shirt joining its brothers as she hung it on the nearest kitchen cabinet. The sound of her soft singing or humming was the background ambience for all these activities.

When finished, with the shirts all hung neatly in place and the kitchen table covered with piles of neatly folded articles, she would declare, "Well, finished for another week." Once she put her equipment away, she would carry my father's clothing upstairs to the bedroom. Everything that was on a hanger, she would put away. Anything that needed to go into a drawer, she would leave for him to put away. Again, I don't know why; this was just their routine.

When my father came home, she would tell him immediately, "Thurston, your clothes are on your bed ready for you to put away."

"Okay, Sweetpea [his nickname for her], thank you." And upstairs he would go to put his clothes away. Each of them seemed satisfied with the day's events.

I often think about my parents' marriage. When growing up, I never imagined any tender interactions between them, but all these years later here it was.

My father died in 1984. He and my mother had married young and had been married for more than fifty years. They had gone through poverty, separations, and infidelity, and finally had matured together. When I went to visit my mother after his death, I felt I could see both the love that had first attracted them and also the love that had grown as they had grown.

I watched as she showed me how she now organized her day, still with my father as part of it. She would get up in the morning, get dressed, and before having breakfast would have one cup of coffee. Sitting in her comfortable lounger that looked out through a large picture window onto Conemaugh Street, she would first check the weather. She would then change the date on her perpetual calendar, and before taking her first sip of coffee, she would kiss the small photograph of my father that sat on the table beside her chair.

"Good morning, Thurston," she would say, and describe the weather for the day. The softness in her voice convinced me that while I hadn't been able to see it, perhaps some tenderness between them had always been present but just needed the passage of time and the maturity gained with age and experience to grow and flourish.

I realize in writing this story that this is the first time I have ever portrayed my father in any kind of favorable light. He was always the villain and my mother the victim. Not that everything I have described in the past wasn't true; it was. But obviously things slowly changed over the years. That is why, when talking with my sister

Mimsi, who's five years younger than me, we describe very different experiences with my father. She describes someone warmer and much more engaged.

While I can't change the past, perhaps at this stage of my life I can begin to think of my father with some empathy and, yes, even a little tenderness.

Susie and Thurston

Chuckie and Nancy

Nancy, Chuckie, Susie, Judy, Billy, Mimsi and Snip

Mimsi

MOVING ON

Lost in Translation

The gastroenterologist said, "You're only fifty-seven years old and have already had two endoscopies in three months and it's really too soon to do another."

Finally, acquiescing to my tearful pleas, he reluctantly ordered a third test.

He reached me at home as I had left work early on a Friday due to increasing nausea and general weakness.

"I'm sorry, Nancy, but you have esophageal cancer. We need to start treatment immediately. Monday is July Fourth, a holiday, but I've made an appointment for you with an oncologist at Norris Hospital on Tuesday. I am truly sorry."

What he really meant was, you are about to experience the most terrifying journey of your life. Not everyone who makes this journey survives.

The compassionate female oncologist said, "We will treat you with our protocol, which is a combination of chemotherapy and radiation for six weeks, after which you will be scheduled for surgery. Side effects from this regimen could include nausea, vomiting, fatigue, hair loss, and lesions in your mouth, which is called mucositis. Some months after surgery, you will have a second round of chemotherapy to prevent reoccurrence. I must tell you that even with this treatment, the survival rate is only five percent."

What she really meant was, you will have a catheter surgically implanted in your chest, which will then be attached to a medication-filled fanny pack to facilitate your receiving a toxic drug called 5-FU. Weekly, you will have an additional infusion of another agent called Leucovorin. This was to be a six-hour procedure done in the outpatient treatment center at Norris Hospital. The nausea from these combined treatments will be so intense you will be reluctant to move. Lying on your sofa at home, waiting for the pharmacy to deliver your Kytril to alleviate the nausea, you will try to not even blink, hoping that if you are still enough, the waves of nausea will subside. Everyday odors will suddenly seem noxious to you. Losing your hair will be an unnerving process as your hair falls out in clumps so that you resemble a dog with mange. Your brother-in-law will finally shave your head so that you will no longer start your day by awakening to spider-like clusters of hair lying on the pillow beside you. You will feel badly when your daughter proudly makes you a protein-filled smoothie from fresh peaches, as she knows peaches are your favorite, but you can't drink it because the acidity burns the lesions in your mouth caused by mucositis. You will appreciate the foresight of having spent money on a new Tempur-Pedic mattress and a new Bose CD player as you will spend most of your time in bed trying to lose yourself in the music. Years later, you will still react when you hear certain jazz songs played and/or sung by certain jazz artists, because hearing these songs takes you back to those difficult times. You will meet a woman by the name of Joanne who is apparently on the same radiation treatment schedule as you. You do not become friends per se, rather just two women who smile wanly and acknowledge each other's presence as you report for your daily radiation treatments. Joanne even has surgery scheduled on the same day as you.

The cardiothoracic surgeon said, "This will be a twelve-hour surgery. We will first position you on your side so I may do a thoracotomy to reach the necessary organs I must manipulate from your right side. Once completed, you will then be positioned on your back to allow me to make an incision that will start just below your throat. I will complete the surgery from this area. When you awaken, you will have many lines. An indwelling catheter, an IV, three abdominal drains, and blood if necessary. We will treat your pain with an epidural. Nursing staff will get you out of bed the day after surgery and every day for the next two weeks until you are discharged. It's a big operation, but I'm confident that you can get through this."

What he really meant was that I would awaken and gradually become aware of the multiple lines; the IV, the three small bottle-shaped drains rolling across my abdomen, and the catheter. No blood was actually running. It was late in the day, and I slept. When I awoke the next morning, three nurses assisted me out of bed. Two steadied me and the third managed my many "lines." It was very strange as I could not really tell where my limbs were, especially my legs. My first attempt to get out of bed was a failure due to low blood pressure problems, but subsequent attempts were successful. I had a cough and a random gurgling noise in my throat accompanied by a gulping movement, which would occur without warning. I feared this as it was a constant reminder of my lack of control of so many things. I continued to get out of bed and walk every day although the cough persisted. Soon I was strong enough for physical therapy.

Joanne, who was assigned to the room next to mine, also had a successful surgery, but had no cough, and was recovering nicely.

The physical therapist said, "Even with that cough, you will get stronger before you go home and I'll continue to see you every week even after discharge."

I was discharged after one month, still coughing and on large doses of codeine cough syrup. Joanne had a medical complication and died before I was discharged.

Sometime after discharge, the physical therapist said, "Norris has eleven landings if you start in the basement. Our goal is that we will start in the basement and together we will walk eleven floors to the top! This was one of the few moments of hearty laughter that I can clearly remember, as it seemed ludicrous for me to even try. But of course, I did. We started with one floor at a time. I reached the first landing huffing and puffing and had to sit down and rest before I could recover, get in my car, and drive home. Soon I could do the first landing and we moved on to the second and subsequent landings. He was encouraging and patient, and floor by floor we climbed those eleven stories. On the day I reached the eleventh landing, I sank unbelievingly on the top step and cried. I was recovered and I was strong. I had beaten cancer.

Today, twenty-two years later, it is at times hard for me to believe and relive these events. There are still aftereffects from my surgery, mostly episodes of hoarseness, and I no longer have the vocal range I once had. But I am alive and living a good life. I was one of the lucky five percent.

Nancy McKeever

What Happens in Vegas...

"What? Wait, wait, go back a minute! Did you just say that Thurston Flurry, my father, your father, our father, actually took you shopping for clothes? Alone? More than once? Un-f---ing believable! When did this happen, and how did I not know about it?"

I was speaking to my sister Mimsi, who looked at me with an amused expression.

"Look, Bitchface [her sisterly nickname for me at times], I don't know why you didn't know. Maybe you were living in the nurses' residence by then. He always took me shopping for my winter coat. He would say, 'Mimsi, meet Daddy under the Kaufmann's department store clock at four o'clock. Don't worry if I'm a little late. I have to take the bus from the mill in Homestead all the way to downtown, and it takes a while, but don't worry, Daddy will be there.' Sometimes, on the way home after shopping, we would even stop at Isaly's for ice cream."

"Don't worry, Daddy will be there! Stop at Isaly's!" I was dumbfounded. Who was she talking about?

We were in Vegas just after our first full day of gambling. As usual, we had reserved adjoining rooms. Through the open doors between the two rooms, we could hear my brother-in-law Robert snoring above both

TVs. We were in my room in our nightclothes, each sprawled on one of the queen-size beds. We would talk until we became too sleepy, but never because we ran out of things to discuss.

At home, Mimsi and I talked at least four times a week. No subject was off limits, no holds barred, and no judgments made. We were always completely honest with each other, and I thought I knew everything about her. I was only five years older, but I had begun caring for her at a very young age. She was born two months after the death of an older sibling who died when he was only eleven months old. My mother was then thirty-three, and Mimsi was her seventh child. Married to a known philanderer and often absentee father, my mother must have been severely depressed, with very little support from her husband. Despite the unrelenting pressures of racism, poverty, loss, and a precarious marital status, my mother never neglected us in any way. She remained as present as possible, but I was the one, under her supervision, who dressed Mimsi, combed her hair, saw that she got her share of our meager meals, entertained her as best I could, and acted as the referee between her and Judy.

In my first truly clear memory of Mimsi and me, I'm eight and she's three. I've dressed her for Easter in a new pink dress with puffy sleeves, a lace-like bodice, and a softly flared skirt, all tied with a large bow. White socks and scuffed black shoes burnished with a small application of Vaseline completed her outfit. I proudly walk her around our block even though I, perhaps already fulfilling the role of the selfless, uncomplaining "good girl" of the family, am wearing a hand-me-down dress from my older sister Snip, worn orthopedic shoes, and pink-plastic-framed county-issued glasses. Mimsi has no memory of that day.

She grew into a five-foot-nine teenager by age thirteen while I was off to nursing school. During this period, she reminded me of a giraffe—tall, with long slender legs and skin the color of warm caramel. She also had a giraffe's expression, towering over everyone else with disdain. That animal has a presence that says "Step aside, I'm here!" I thought the same of Mimsi. Somehow, when you saw her, you knew she was a force to be reckoned with. Unlike me, she gave her opinion, whether asked or not. Although she got shorter and heavier as she aged, Mimsi's approach to life remains unchanged. She moved through the world like an entitled queen. Walking through the airport with her on our trips to Vegas, I could feel the crowds part like a herd of wild animals as this statuesque woman made her way to the gate with her husband and I allowed her to clear the path ahead of us.

During my years of living in the nurses' residence, she called often to keep me updated on life in school and at home. After graduating from high school, and against my father's strong objections, Mimsi went to live with my older sister Shirley, her three children, and her husband who was stationed in the Air Force in Merced, California. We kept in touch by phone and by letters. This is how I learned of their eventual move to Los Angeles, her meeting Robert, and their subsequent plans to marry despite my older sister's disapproval. I missed Mimsi's wedding because she moved up the date due to my older sister's negative behavior. Forty-seven years of marriage, with both ups and downs, as in any relationship, has proven my older sister's assessment incorrect.

My first trip to Vegas was with Mimsi and Robert. I didn't know if I'd like it, knew nothing about gambling, and couldn't imagine spending a whole day sitting in front of a slot machine. My, how quickly things can change. We have now been to Vegas numerous times and in various configurations: all four sisters and Robert, my sister-in-law and me and Mimsi and Robert; my daughter, Mimsi's daughter, me, Mimsi, and Robert; and finally, just the three of us. We have decided that this configuration works best for us and jealously guard our travel plans. At six-foot-four, the color of Hershey bar chocolate, and built like a football player, Robert watched over us in Vegas as if he had two wives. However, when I overstepped my bounds and tried to tell him what to bet or not bet, he gently reminded me that he only had one wife and that was not me. We got along well and he was very protective of his nosy sister-in-law.

So here we were in our usual places, making plans for the next day of gambling.

"Hey, you realize none of us won anything today," I said.

"You say that every time," Mimsi answered, "and then on the last day, you can't lose! So just shut up! But like Daddy used to say, another day, another dollar."

"Daddy used to say a lot of things, my dear," I reminded her. "Some true and some not."

"I know he could be a pain in the ass," she responded, "but he didn't usually give me a hard time if I handled him right. When he referred to me as Mimi, I knew I was okay."

And that's when she dropped the bomb about the shopping. I was speechless. I could not imagine going shopping with my father. Him taking the time to meet me in a department store after work and waiting to buy me anything! What would that have looked like? What would we have talked about? Wouldn't he have been his usual abrupt and impatient self? And I knew I would have been my usual be-a-good-girl-and-hurry-up-and-please-don't-get-Daddy-mad self.

"He treated me differently," she continued. "Maybe

it was because I was the baby, or hell, maybe by that time he was just tired. Two wives and God knows how many kids. Maybe that was too much even for him!"

"What else did he do that I didn't know about?" I asked. I still found it hard to believe that I, of all people, didn't know everything there was to know about Mimsi. And now, in our seventies, I was discovering a significant difference in our perception of our relationship with our father.

"Well," she continued, "first of all, Judy had to tell me who he was. For the longest time, he was just a man who came sometimes in the afternoon and brought a Hershey bar for me, and chocolate-covered cherries for Momma, and she would smile and hold his hand." She went on, "He used to walk me to Sunday school some weeks and he would never say no if I asked for a new dress or something. He might say 'Daddy doesn't have the money right now, baby.' But in a few days, Momma, never Daddy, would give me money and say 'This is from your father for your...whatever.'"

I lay there in amazement. She was truly describing someone I didn't know.

"How is it possible that we talk all the time, and I didn't know all this?"

"I don't know, because to me it was just normal. I don't remember him being especially mean or anything.

I know he had his moods, but as long as he called me Mimi or referred to me as the baby, I knew things were fine between us."

"I guess sometimes it's better not to remember," she said, shaking her head.

We ended the night on that note.

I thought about this conversation long after we returned to L.A. Did it bother me? Was I jealous? Was I angry because I missed these experiences with my father? Did I think he loved her more? Was it because she was the baby? When I sobbed at his funeral, was I crying for what I wished we had had together but never did? I wondered if he recognized in Mimsi the same "don't mess with me" attitude that he had. Kindred souls, maybe?

While I truly didn't feel upset or angry, I did wish things had been different between us. It's very difficult to grow up fearing your father, always having to be hyper-vigilant, feeling the need to interpret his every move: the way he entered the house when he returned from work, his stance as he went through the doorway, his tone of voice, the way he said my name, and never being able to relax lest some minor infraction on someone's part (usually one of the girls) triggered a violent verbal reaction.

It is true that my father softened with age and became a warmer husband and father, and a doting grandfather. He even fondly referred to me as his Nancy

Nurse, his initial objections to my attending school seemingly forgotten.

It feels as if we had different fathers housed in the same body. Yet doesn't every sibling in any family have a different perspective of their parents and experiences? After all, my experience is only my experience. Albeit all of it validated by my older siblings, most of us separated by two years but Mimsi and me by five. Is birth order the explanation?

I didn't know the answer to these questions but accepted that our experiences differed. Perhaps that was what these unexpected moments were meant for: a chance to discover more about myself, Mimsi, our childhood, and the world in general. Who knows what revelations the giraffe will share on our next trip to Vegas?

Nancy McKeever

Every Picture Tells a Story

The photo has hung on my refrigerator for fifteen years, and on yet another refrigerator for fifteen years before that. There was a time when looking at it triggered feelings of resentment and anger directed toward my mother, who I had revered all my life.

I always thought my mother was perfect, a saint. In fact, sometimes in jest and at times with just a bit of sarcasm, my siblings and I called her Saint Susie. She was someone who always did and said the right thing to please everyone no matter the situation or circumstance. Even under the quadruple-pronged burden of poverty, racism, sexism, and marital infidelity, she managed to successfully raise six children, each one believing they were special and each one believing "Momma" could resolve any dilemma to everyone's satisfaction. Thus, when she and I spoke about why she made a decision that so negatively impacted us sisters living in California, I was truly confused. Why couldn't she just do what she had always done? Resolve the situation in her usual saintly way to everyone's satisfaction? At forty-seven years old, I was only beginning to recognize the burden that "sainthood" placed both on the sainted and the devotee.

The photo on my refrigerator is of my brother

Chuckie and me. Chuckie, two years older than me, dark-skinned, tall and rail-thin with high cheekbones and usually sporting a wide smile that revealed the gap between his two front teeth just like Saint Susie and all his siblings. Chuckie, who had intervened in the sexual abuse by my Uncle Walter when I was eight, continued to protect me as I learned to navigate the subtle nuances of maintaining popularity in both junior high and high school, and later helped ease the toll of an ill-fated marriage.

He had once lived in Los Angeles, but when that photo was taken he had been living and working in Rochester, New York, where he was Western Regional Director for the Xerox Corporation. He was a man with voracious appetites who loved life. Loved dressing well, loved music and dancing, loved to cook (his specialty was pineapple upside-down cake), and loved to eat. He traveled to L.A. often, but definitely every Thanksgiving, when he spent the day visiting each of his three sisters' homes and having a full meal at each house. I once watched as he left my house, placed a postprandial piece of sweet potato pie on his car roof while he folded his lanky frame into his shiny metallic gray Nissan 380Z, reached a long, skinny arm out the car window to snatch the pie from the car roof, then zoomed off on his way to my younger sister Mimsi's house. He remained skinny as a rail until he became ill.

In the photo, we're standing side by side, his left arm draped over my left shoulder, my right arm halfway around his waist. Pink sponge curlers march neatly around my entire head and I'm wearing what was then my favorite sleeping attire, a red cotton nightshirt with a picture of the dancing California Raisins on the front with the words *I heard it through the grapevine* emblazoned over their heads. Chuckie is neatly dressed in a black turtleneck, green shirt, and black pants. A small but familiar smile is present in his no longer smooth dark face, the skin on it now covered in deep purple bruises, the familiar sign of Kaposi's sarcoma, a cancer found in AIDS patients. His once-slim torso is now bloated with abdominal edema, causing his stomach to hang slightly over his belt. He holds a coffee cup in his right hand. His last cup before leaving for the airport to return to Rochester that morning. That would be his last visit to L.A.

It had been approximately a year since he had informed the entire family of his AIDS diagnosis. In a detailed letter sent simultaneously to all of us, he made us aware of his diagnosis and probable prognosis, offering to answer any questions we might have. He and I had a few conversations about his illness and lifestyle, but listening to his descriptions of bath houses and his use of "poppers" was truthfully more information than I wanted to have. We discussed instead his daily life, how long he thought he could work, and his will, in which he included specific details about steps to take in seeking his children, who had disappeared along with his wife when he had come out publicly. As his illness progressed and he could no longer travel to L.A., he continued to visit my parents as often as he could in Pittsburgh.

When he became too ill to travel, the California and Pittsburgh family members would take turns making the trip to Rochester to visit him in his home, where he was able to remain with the assistance of an in-home aide. Once Chuckie was hospitalized, we tried to visit more frequently. I vividly remember once entering his hospital room and finding his cold, untouched breakfast tray sitting on the bedside table very near to the door and definitely out of his reach, with his also cold, untouched lunch tray sitting beside it. This was 1989, and many people in and out of hospitals were still reluctant to come in contact with AIDS patients.

Chuckie died on September 19, 1989.

Not unexpected but still distressing and painfully sad. He was just forty-nine years old.

Preparations for his funeral began immediately, and they proved to be long, complicated, and frustrating. Because of the AIDS diagnosis, my older brother

Billy had to maneuver his way through what seemed like endless miles of red tape to make arrangements for Chuckie's body to be flown from Rochester to Pittsburgh.

Every day there were many phone calls going back and forth between both coasts.

"When is the funeral, Momma? Do you have any idea? We need to make arrangements for time off work, buy plane tickets, etc."

"I'll let you know as soon as I know for sure," my mother would say.

I knew from my older brother that she was having a difficult time with my father who, true to form, refused to discuss the topic of his gay son and his diagnosis with her or anyone.

My mother called me one Thursday evening. I had just gotten home from work but was eager, as always, to talk with her.

"Your brother's body finally got here yesterday. I want you and your sisters to know that the funeral is tomorrow morning at 11."

"Tomorrow! Momma, why tomorrow? We can't possibly get there in time. Why is it so soon? Did you forget about us?"

"Oh honey, it has been such a mess. Getting the body here and trying to make arrangements. As soon as people hear the cause of death, everything becomes a problem."

She continued, "And it's so hard on your father. He's not doing well at all, Not talking and hardly eating. Both his diabetes and blood pressure are out of control!"

"Momma," I said, choking back the full force of my anger, "it's hard on him because he doesn't want to admit that Chuckie was gay. He doesn't want anyone to know he had a gay son, so my brother is going to be buried quickly with three of his sisters missing his funeral. I know you're trying to take care of everyone including Daddy but it's just not right!"

By this time, we were crying; both of us grappling with anger, frustration, and sadness. We finally ended the conversation, with her signing off with what up until now had been her usually comforting words.

"Remember, Momma loves you."

"I love you too, Momma."

The truth of these words sounded painfully incongruent with the conversation that had just ended. I spent the morning of my brother's funeral 2,500 miles away with my sister Mimsi; reminiscing, crying, and laughing as we remembered my brother, a private funeral of two.

Though we continued to remain in close contact, it was months before I asked my mother about the specifics of Chuckie's funeral. She had never offered any details and I had not asked. I think it was too painful and shameful for both of us. There we were, a grieving mother who had lost a second son, was emotionally estranged from her husband over this event, and whose relationship with three of her four daughters was also strained. And I, a sister grieving for her brother and even more so over the fact that Saint Susie had not performed her usual miracle. All of us had expected her to make everything work for everyone as she always had in the past.

Given time, of course, we did discuss it. My mother described the shame that accompanied the hurried burial, the lies about Chuckie having pneumonia, and my father's reluctant attendance at his son's funeral and his continued taciturn and unsupportive behavior.

"But that was my son," she said, her voice tight with anguish.

I, in turn, after apologizing for my anger and insensitivity for her predicament, told her how Mimsi and I had spent the day together, and she seemed pleased that we had done so. Over time the pain for all of us eased.

Over the years, of course the pain and anger and sadness for us all has faded. Thank goodness the photograph itself has not. Now I look at the photo with sadness as two of the main characters in this story are gone; however, I no longer feel any rancor toward my mother; only acceptance and understanding and love. At the age of 47, I had to give up the fantasy that my mother was a saint. I acknowledged the fact that she had proven over and over throughout her life and mine that she was as perfect as any mother could be.

Nancy McKeever

Invictus

He stood in the den with his back to the kitchen. Though dressed casually, his stance was one of someone in full dress uniform. Six feet tall, his ramrod straight posture made him appear even taller than he actually was. Standing at attention, chin slightly elevated, eyes looking straight ahead through the sliding glass doors that framed the red, purple, and orange bougainvillea vines that cascaded down the sides of the garage, he spoke in a clear strong voice:

> *Out of the night that covers me,*
> *Black as the pit from pole to pole,*
> *I thank whatever gods may be*
> *For my unconquerable soul.*

Gesticulating to emphasize certain points, you could tell from his inflection that he knew these words well and had spoken them many times before. My brother Billy was reciting the poem "Invictus" by William Ernest Henley I had heard him recite many times before. While the origins of how he first learned this poem are unclear, everyone agrees that he was taught this by my mother when he was very young, loved it, and adopted it as a description of life from his perspective. He recited this poem whenever the mood struck him, with the passion of one who truly believes in the words he is saying. It was such a part of him and his life that he was even asked to recite it at a friend's funeral. The message of "Invictus" is the deep-rooted ability to display fortitude in the face of adversity. It describes unwavering courage and determination.

It seems such a fitting poem for my brother, and maybe he knew intuitively at a young age that this poem reflected the challenges he would meet in life. The oldest of seven children and the offspring of a sometimes absentee father, he very early in life developed a strong sense of family responsibility. He was definitely the father figure for all of us. It was to him that I went looking for solutions, whether that meant solving a problem in geometry or deciding how to convince my father to allow me to go to a party unaccompanied by my brother Chuckie. It was Billy who listened to our complaints about our misogynistic father, and facilitated family meetings to try to ease some of the tension that permeated our household. He supported and encouraged my admission into nursing school even though he knew my father strongly disapproved. When I was newly married and attending night school while working, Billy still understood and supported my wish to further my education. When possible, he would slip me spending money, never mentioning the fact that my father had stayed true to his word not to "give me a penny" when I chose education over a job.

He worked at the post office while going to night school and earned his degree from the University of Pittsburgh. Hired as Director of Space Management at Pitt, he worked there until his retirement. While this was further proof of his tenacious attitude, perhaps the death of his seventeen-year-old son after being hit by a drunk driver was the most excruciating blow he had to absorb, but move through and absorb it he did. The poem continues:

> *In the fell chance of circumstance*
> *I have not winced nor cried aloud.*
> *Under the bludgeoning of chance*
> *My head is bloody but unbowed.*

I graduated from nursing school. Had two children. Left my husband after eight years. And while my brother and I kept in touch, it was a different relationship. He was now on his second marriage to Margaret, a woman who seemed perfect for him. They worked, then retired, first to Naples, Florida, and then to Ajijic, Mexico. It's a quiet, slow-paced town with a large contingent of expats from Canada and the United States. They enjoyed the warm weather all year round. Billy played tennis three times a week. Each year, they traveled to L.A. so Billy could have a yearly VA visit and continue monitoring his Crohn's disease, which has plagued him most of his life but seemed to settle down with their move to idyllic Ajijic. Stress relief is a cure for many things.

It was during these yearly visits that I had the chance to establish an adult relationship with my brother. We would spend time together teasing, reminiscing, and laughing as he filled our home with his magnetic presence. Our relationship deepened and became richer as we discussed the ways in which our lives were different yet still the same. Even after all these years, he remained my big brother, my hero. Everything we did together was an adventure. He and Margaret always came with a long shopping list, as there were various items that were not easily available in Mexico. It was a treat to shop with them. No matter what type of business we entered, by the time we were leaving, everyone in the establishment knew Billy and treated him as if he were a lifelong customer. It was amazing to watch and to be a part of.

At some point in each visit, "Invictus" would be spontaneously triggered and recited, the trigger known only to Billy.

Some years ago, they decided to obtain their medical care in Mexico, so the yearly visits to L.A. ended. We stayed in touch, but it was just not the same. The closeness and special intimacy was gone, and sorely missed. Then Billy suffered a series of medical events including prostate problems, a pacemaker implantation, a ruptured bowel, and the subsequent need for a colostomy and a tracheostomy. His condition was dire, and I had to face the fact that my beloved brother could die. His medical status was unpredictable from December to March, when he finally came home from the hospital for the last time.

After weeks of debating if and when I should see him, I finally traveled there for a visit. Entering my brother's bedroom for the first time was shocking. There he was in ninety-degree weather, wrapped in his bed linens, with a knitted cap on his head. He was painfully thin. All I could do was kneel by his bed, put my head on his bony chest, and cry while he gently touched my head and joined in my tears.

I spent my time there visiting in a way we had never visited before. My brother, who had always been the personification of strength and courage, talked easily of weakness, dependence, sickness, and mortality. Historically, in our family, the tendency had been to deny what was happening as it occurred. Prostate problems? Oh, that's common and easily taken care of. Placement of a pacemaker? Oh, that's done all the time. No need to worry. By the time Billy got to the tracheostomy and the ruptured bowel, the denial was harder to maintain. The issue of mortality hung over us like a vulture circling its weakening prey. He would have good days, then bad. Various infections invaded his body and did not seem to respond to antibiotics. There was even a discussion of arranging to medevac him to the VA in Los Angeles. No one knew the right thing to do.

By the time I saw him, all medical treatment and devices had been discontinued except for his colostomy, which could be reversed at a later date. The focus was on nutrition and physical therapy. I'd like to think my visit helped as I started cooking on the day I landed in Ajijic. He requested, and received, fried fish, macaroni and cheese, spaghetti, pork chops, sweet potato pie, and other favorite foods. He started wearing his hearing aids, which he had not worn since December. The progress was very slow but encouraging.

The three of us talked about his continued struggle, and both he and Margaret (and I agreed with them) considered this illness their "Invictus" and were determined to conquer it. Billy continued to improve daily. He became stronger and began eating well. Since he had always loved to cook, this was integrated into his daily physical therapy routine.

I saw a video of him making pancakes. Margaret had

gotten very good at taking videos and keeping me abreast of his progress. I watched as he struggled to complete the simplest task with fierce determination. Obviously tired and stopping at intervals to rest, he pushed himself. It was as if he was in a battle and his most formidable challenger was himself. I watched him on the videos and thought of our tearful parting when I left him and how much progress he had made in that time. I thought of the last verse of the poem and knew that the words would keep him going as they had for all his life.

It matters not how strait the gate,
How charged with punishments the scroll,
I am the master of my fate
I am the captain of my soul.

And Then There Were Three

Still half asleep, I stepped into the warm shower and reached for the body wash. Liberally soaping up, I casually examined the articles on the over-the-showerhead caddy. Not much to see except one bottle of Dove body wash, one bath sponge, and one razor, which on closer examination appeared ready to be discarded. Oh yes, and a huge brush for scrubbing your back, which belonged to Bayla, whom you will meet shortly. Turning to allow the water to stream down my back, I examined the tall shower caddy in the back corner that Bayla uses, a three-shelf contraption that fit nicely in the corner and was crammed full of at least twenty hair and bath products. Some neatly placed, some not, and many with very eye-catching names like Blueberry Bliss and Drunken Elephant, the names giving no clue as to the use of any particular product. Drunken Elephant? Now what could that be for? I didn't take the time to determine any uses but could only think, who would even have the time to apply all those various potions?

Bayla Raine Borquez is Patty's twenty-year-old niece, who was born in Los Angeles but moved with her family to Tehachapi when she was two. Seeking a better life for their four children, the Borquezes moved to escape from the hustle, bustle, and crime of the big city. Relocating from a house in L.A., they moved into a sprawling farm complete with horses, pigs, chickens, and sheep—just like Old MacDonald. Three generations occupied the house. Bayla's mother and father, her older sister Sierra, her younger brother Diego, and the baby, Maya, six years younger. Bayla's maternal grandmother and grandfather lived upstairs in an adjoining area of the huge house.

    I first met the family when Maya was barely two years old. Patty and I drove to Tehachapi one wintry day when there was snow on the ground. I remember little Maya sitting easily in my arms, even though she had just met me, while we watched through the dining room window as their father led the three older children on a sled ride on the side of their house. Later, I watched as Maya danced with her grandfather in front of the giant fireplace in the "quiet room," her small two-year-old feet placed on her grandpa's feet so she could dance with him. They resembled a Norman Rockwell painting.

    Despite this idyllic picture, Bayla always knew that she wanted to eventually leave the quiet town of Tehachapi. When making plans for graduation from high school, she also knew that she was not quite ready to make the leap from Tehachapi to the University of Washington, where she eventually hoped to go. Santa

Monica College was a possible bridge.

Having spent many summers in Santa Monica growing up, she was at least familiar with the city and as familiar with our house as she was with her own. And so, after many discussions between Bayla, her parents, Patty, and me, the decision was made that she would live with us and attend Santa Monica College. Not that there weren't questions. I had already raised three girls; was I up to the task again? Would I actually be raising her at this age? What was the task, and how did I fit in? After all, she was eighteen. I wasn't her mother and didn't want to be a mother! Part of Patty's reasoning was that it would be fun to have a lively teenager in the house. I had to decide if I wanted additional liveliness or if our sixty- and sixty-seven-year-old liveliness was enough for me. We had many discussions about expectations, daily routines, and division of household responsibilities, with the final outcome of all parties agreeing that we would give this a try.

So we opened our doors and our hearts to this initially shy, quiet eighteen-year-old. Bayla described herself as Latina; her father is Hispanic and her mother white. She is five-foot-three and has long brown hair so dark that it sometimes looks black. It begins with a distinct widow's peak and then cascades like a wavy, silken veil to the middle of her back. The addition of a deep dimple in her right cheek adds to her distinct attractiveness.

Bayla had her own bedroom, of course, decorated exactly to her girlish specifications with the help of her devoted father and his equally devoted credit card. When completed, the room looked like it belonged to a princess, and because of this, I dubbed her Queen B. Because of factors that included her age, school, work, and an active social life, the room soon deteriorated into Queen B's own special brand of teenage chaos. I thought of the huge bedroom that both of my daughters and Heather shared in their teenage years. I was very big on them keeping it reasonably neat and clean and wondered now, when looking at Bayla's mound of clean (or maybe dirty) clothes piled on a chair, various books and papers scattered on the floor, and multiple pairs of shoes marching around her bed, why it didn't bother me. Was it because I didn't feel responsible, or was I learning to discriminate between what was really important and what was less so? I found it all rather amusing and wondered how, in all this disarray, she managed to emerge on time for school and work each day neat, clean, and appropriately dressed. Did that mean that I had been too hard on my children unnecessarily? Too late to change any of that, I thought. Now, twice Bayla's age, they seemed to be fairly well-adjusted women, we were all still speaking, we saw each other regularly, and our conversations still ended with "Love you!" With all of this being true, I decided to just let the past go and let the present flow at will. If I was disturbed by something or felt my space was being invaded, it would be discussed. Other than that, we were a newly created family learning how to live together in relative peace.

Bayla seemed to understand fairly quickly that she would often get an echo of the same message, maybe only a few minutes apart, from Patty and me. If I reminded her that it was trash day, in ten minutes Patty could be delivering the same message. There was a lot of "Patty already told me," or "Yes, Nancy reminded me already," but it got to be a joke, a family joke. There were, of course, some bumps in the road. Bayla "forgetting to call" when she was going to be out very late. Patty feeling at times that my expectations were too high while I thought hers were not high enough. This had been true when my best friend Esther and I were parenting our three girls, so I tried to approach these situations with a different attitude than that of the Nancy of thirty-five years ago. I realized that some things I would have done differently and some I would have handled exactly the same. But, as with all good families, we worked out our differences and were better for it.

It had been decided early on that Bayla and I would share the larger bathroom, the one with the shower I enjoyed so much, as opposed to the smaller shower off the master bedroom. "This side is yours," I told her. "All this space can be filled with what you need. I'm just asking that the areas be kept separate. All your necessities on your side [including more of the Drunken Elephant, whatever it was] and we'll use my antique mirror as our dividing line." This seemed to work.

As I wrote this, my side of the sink had toothpaste, mouthwash, hand soap, lotion, and assorted candles. Bayla's side had all those same items plus twenty-seven (I actually counted them) additional bottles of various toiletries and hair products. Again, I had no problem with this and found it easy to accept this was her way; however, I would not in a million years confess this to my now-grown daughters.

The most gratifying gift of all had nothing to do with space, boundaries, or chores. It was the unexpected niceties that came with living with her. It was being aware that as we exited the car, she was monitoring the terrain so I didn't trip or stumble, something I initially resented ("She acts like I'm an old lady"), but now appreciate for what it is. Her brand of protectiveness. I loved it when she went shopping and came home excited about sharing her purchases with me. I was immediately transported back many years to enjoying the same activity with one of my older three. An occasional unexpected cooked dinner or a delicious smoothie in the afternoon (one for her and one for me.) It was even pleasurable and most rewarding when she approached me with questions about her homework. Not asking for answers but thinking aloud, voicing her opinions, accepting or rejecting my suggestions, and feeling comfortable in doing so. Together we would reach a compromise acceptable to both of us. Many hours, but so rewarding to again feel needed in this way. Sometimes she was more quiet and moody than at other times. When she wanted to be left alone, I understood and appreciated that because I also felt that way at times. I think this was part of our intuitiveness that let her know it was okay for her, book in hand, to quietly climb into my bed with me and without saying a word, join me in savoring some interesting book of the moment.

I think the three of us have come a long way. I asked Bayla, after it was brought to my attention, if she felt more comfortable, more confident, as if she was coming into her own as a person. If she was proud of her progress in school and her straight A status.

"Yes," she said confidently, without hesitation.

And me, what I have I learned over these almost three years? First, I've learned to relax and to let life lead me where I should go and accept that things will not always go as planned. I've learned that you receive love in many different forms from unexpected sources and in unexpected places. That the real pleasures of life are things such as one of those unexpected homemade smoothies when you're writing in the middle of the afternoon. The gift, for no reason, of a candle that crackles like a real fire simply because that person knows you love that sound and thought of you when out shopping. A candle and a card given to me the day before a procedure, wishing me good luck and saying, "You light up my life" is more meaningful than a dozen roses on Valentine's Day.

Bayla will be leaving in July, although her presence and what she has taught me about myself will remain. I will think of her every time I see that bare bathroom counter or light a candle every day, as I have now gotten into the habit of doing. Her presence will linger in ways I have yet to discover and the memories will make me smile. I hope I have helped her to see that she is strong, smart, capable, and confident, and has a multitude of possibilities awaiting her as she continues on her life's journey.

Once she leaves, the back bathroom caddy will probably remain bare with no trace of any Drunken Elephant, but the new and unanticipated space carved in my heart by her over these past three years will remain, bursting with love and pride for my Queen B.

Sweet Potato Pie

The list, written in pencil, is on an index card that has been handled so many times that the writing appears faint and the notes are scattered haphazardly. I can tell that I was writing in a hurry, trying to get every word down correctly. I smile remembering the conversation between my mother and me. It was November and the start of the holiday season for my family. We had experienced so many scanty holidays during our childhood that as adults we were trying to "make up" for all those years. So, starting with Thanksgiving, we went full-throttle, carrying out what had now become our family traditions, sprinting eagerly toward the finish line of Christmas.

One example of a clear harbinger of the approaching holiday season was the making of sweet potato pie at Thanksgiving, a clear sign that the holiday season had officially begun. We all agreed that my mother was the undisputed star when it came to the baking of sweet potato pie. Fully accepting this title, my mother fulfilled her "duties" by making a sweet potato pie for each family who remained in Pittsburgh. On the Tuesday before Thanksgiving, a pie would be waiting and one could pick it up at will. I loved to pick mine up on that Tuesday, when the house was still bathed in the mouthwatering, nose-pleasing aroma of yams, vanilla, butter, and sugar. Those scents, along with the other less pungent ones of salt, condensed milk, and eggs greeted you as soon as you stepped over the threshold. It wrapped you in a warmth that made you feel like a young child enveloped in the warmth of a mother's love. My mother, proud of the day's accomplishments, would be sitting in her favorite chair, humbly accepting all accolades with a smile on her face. Every year she said the same thing: "I hope they turned out right, but you never know. Let me know."

All of us reacted in the same way by immediately cutting into "our pie" and pronouncing it the best one ever!

This system worked for many years, until my oldest and youngest sisters moved to Los Angeles, followed two years later by me, my two daughters, my best friend, and her daughter. We moved in July and the move seemed to be a successful one until November rolled around. November and the start of our holiday season. A holiday season that was usually heralded by a phone call from my mother announcing when our pies would be ready for pickup. But of course, there was no call, as my mother remained in wintry Pittsburgh and we were in sunny California sans sweet potato pie! I'm still not sure how it was that I was selected to be the baker of that year's pies. With strong encouragement from my sisters, I agreed to call my mother, get her recipe, and yes, bake the pies for Thanksgiving. After our usual pleasantries, the conversation with my mother went something like this:

"Momma, I'm going to try and make sweet potato pie for all of us for Thanksgiving, but I don't have your recipe."

Momma: "Who is 'all of us,' baby?"

Me: "Me, Mim, and Snip. It won't seem like Thanksgiving without a pie. I know it won't be like yours, but I'll follow your recipe closely and we'll see."

There was more than a moment of silence before my mother spoke again.

"I'm sure you can do it but, baby [long pause], I don't have a recipe. I can give you a list of what I use, but it's not like I can tell you two cups of sugar or a cup of condensed milk. Let's start with a list of ingredients and we'll see if I can help."

Thus was born The List.

Momma: "Yams, of course."

Me: "How many yams, Momma? Two for each pie, or more?"

Momma: "Well, I guess you could start with two for each pie, but you have to go with the way the batter looks and feels. You'll know."

Momma: "Next, eggs."

Me: "Another two per pie? Does that sound right?"

Momma: "Well, why don't you just start with that and keep checking on that batter. That's important! Next, you'll need some sugar, and you just sweeten the batter to taste. That's easy."

Me: "Uh-huh, something easy, thank goodness! Look, Sue [we called her by her first name whenever we wanted to irritate her or maybe when she was irritating us!]. Since there doesn't seem to be any real measurements, why don't you just give me the full list and anything else you want to tell me?"

Momma: "Alright baby, here's everything you need: Yams, butter, sugar, eggs, lots of vanilla, salt, and condensed milk. Mix everything together and make sure it's soupy...that's the secret."

Me: "Soupy?"

Momma: "Yes, soupy, and it will firm up as it bakes. It's not complicated, baby; you can do it. Just keep checking on that batter, making sure it looks and feels right to you."

And so, with these directions, I tried that first year, only to create a disastrous mess. A pie that was so bad I wouldn't even let my sisters taste it. I had tried to make some sense of how much of each ingredient was called for and failed, and even though my final batter's consistency was what I would call soupy, the final result was of a thick pasty texture that caught in my throat when I tried to swallow. My older sister gave up on me immediately, while my younger sister encouraged me to try again. With less disastrous results the second year, I allowed my younger sister to taste it and though she pronounced it "not too bad," to me that meant that I obviously still had a long way to go. My mother also kept track of my attempts and failures, telling me to relax and promising that my efforts would eventually be rewarded.

My third, and what I had decided would be my last, attempt was a rousing success that I still cannot explain. Astonishingly, this would not be my best sweet potato pie, as with every passing year they improved. Somehow, I grew in confidence. It felt like a miracle.

"I knew you could do it!" my mother said.

For the next many years, I made pie at Thanksgiving for my younger sister and me; none for my doubting older sister who chose to do without rather than admit to my achievement. I had accepted the challenge of achieving a mouthwatering sweet potato pie and I prevailed.

That should have been the happy ending to this story, but it was not. Patty and I moved to an independent living facility for seniors, a facility that provides all meals and actively encourages you not to cook but to eat from their kitchen. Keeping that "no cooking" edict in mind, before our move, we gave away our large pot that was perfect for cooking yams, and our hand mixer that was perfect for bringing the ingredients to a soupy consistency. Although we have a refrigerator, microwave, and two burners that work fine for cooking small things, we have no oven. November and Thanksgiving fast approached, bringing with it the craving for a delicious sweet potato pie. And while our living facility's Thanksgiving menu is described as "a delectable array of delights including ham, turkey, stuffing, gravy, sweet potatoes, eggs Benedict, bacon, sausage, assorted pastries, and more," you can see from that list that it does not include sweet potato pie. To address this appalling lapse in judgment, we discussed the possibility of borrowing a large pot from our old housekeeper, a hand mixer from my wonderful sister, and most importantly, another resident offered the use of her toaster oven, which she says, under her guidance, can bake anything! Question: Should I accept this new sweet potato pie challenge or not? Hmm, I wonder.

Yay Parade

My cell phone rang at exactly 11 a.m. If I had been a little more cognizant of the date and time, I might have guessed who it was even before I saw my sister Mimsi's face appear on the screen.

"I'm just calling to make sure you know that today is November first, and you know what that means. The Christmas shopping season has officially started, and you can't buy anything for yourself until after Christmas unless it is an absolute necessity!"

I laughed and said, "Okay, Mrs. Claus, and before you say anything else, yes, I'll remind my daughters."

"Now that that's settled," she continued, "what's going on?"

My sister and I talk every day, and for years this particular Christmas shopping ritual has been our practice. Starting in November you buy nothing for yourself lest you interfere with her picking out a special gift for you. I can't remember how this started, but that's what we do and all family members are aware of this "tradition" and have fallen in line with Aunt Mimsi's dictate. No further reference was made to this subject during subsequent conversations as there was really no need. Everyone knew and everyone complied. If they didn't comply, they certainly kept it to themselves.

We have many traditions connected with Christmas, all geared toward making it a spectacular day in every way. I'm sure that growing up poor and sometimes receiving nothing for Christmas is a huge part of our continued need to make this an extra-special day. And while it may sound materialistic, it really is not so much about receiving gifts. It is about the giving of a special gift to someone you love and seeing the joy reflected on their face when they receive it. So starting in November, family members are encouraged, not browbeaten, into generating a Christmas list. Any reasonable or even slightly unreasonable request is acceptable. One exception to this is that Mimsi and I never exchange lists or even discuss what we might want, but somehow we always manage to surprise and please each other every year.

My two daughters and I, along with Esther and her daughter Heather, have savored more than forty Christmas dinners together, so our routine is set in stone. Even when I moved in with my now partner, Patty; she continued her own tradition of spending Christmas Eve and Christmas Day with her adopted Tehachapi family, and the five of us continued on as before. Patty and I then have a combined Christmas and New Year's celebration with just the two of us.

This year, I started thinking about our traditional

Christmas dinner—honey-baked ham, macaroni and cheese, candied sweet potatoes, kale, rolls, and whatever dessert was decided upon for that year. Heather would supply the appetizers; Stacey always picked up the ham; I cooked the sides; and Nancy Jean made dessert. Esther has been unable to contribute recently due to her Parkinson's, but she's as vocal as everyone else about what is acceptable. Same meal cooked the same way every year.

    Kale was not always trendy. It used to be very cheap and thus very popular with the poorer population. When I was growing up, and even as a young adult with children, you did not find kale at Trader Joe's neatly washed and bagged and ready to cook. No, you bought these huge stalks of kale with their dark green tightly curled leaves, knowing that much preparation was needed prior to cooking. First, each long, leafy stalk had to be washed three times, according to my mother's specification. During the first washing, you looked not only for the obvious dirt (and there was plenty of it), but it was extremely important to check each tightly curled leaf to ensure that a big fat green worm was not snuggled up close to the stalk, which ran the length of the leaf. Curled up and hanging on as if they could delay their demise. When we complained about this tedious task, my mother would say, "Well, if you leave a worm in it, that will just mean more meat for someone." That got us to stop complaining and refocus every time. So one wash for obvious dirt and less obvious but more disgusting worms. A second wash to get anything you missed the first time, and a third wash, as my mother would say, "just to be sure."

The greens were then placed in a huge pot with a piece of pork for seasoning, onions, and a pinch of baking soda, which, again according to my mother, got rid of any bitterness. Placed on the stove they then cooked for hours while their mouthwatering scent permeated the house. The simmering pot caused the December-chilled windows to steam up and somehow made the house seem cozier, as if the walls were arms wrapping the whole house in a warm embrace. While the thorough cleaning we used to do is no longer necessary, I still cook them the same way, and the aroma of greens cooking continues to evoke the comforting feeling of a holiday.

So why, this year, did I think about changing the menu? I had no other specific meal in mind, but I thought maybe it's time for a change, or maybe I just didn't want to cook. I cautiously broached the subject with the ladies. They in turn conveyed through phone calls, emails, texts, and various emojis that they preferred that the menu remain unchanged, thank you very much, and even offered to cook. Well, this was even better. More than I expected. So I took them up on their offer. Somehow

Nancy Jean became the organizer, and I made plans to have a more leisurely Christmas, where I could take my time to decorate and wrap presents. I said to myself when the decision was made, *Yay parade!* This phrase is one that only makes sense to the five of us. When they were very young, my girls often mangled the English language in such a way that it was often hilarious. Instead of Kentucky Fried Chicken, KFC, or Colonel Sanders, Stacey would say Colonel Sandals, as in footwear. If someone blew their horn at us, she would say, "Why is that man hornin' at us?" They also called the UPS truck the "ups truck." Heather was indignant as only a teenager can be when she learned they had been mispronouncing it all their lives.

All of these sayings were a source of amusement over the years, but gradually fell out of use as the girls grew older. Heather's contribution, which has stayed with us, was this: When something especially good would happen, when we wanted the girls to be excited, we would say "Hip, hip, hurray!" to signify that this was something to cheer about, that an adventure was about to happen! What Heather heard, however, was not "Hip, hip, hurray!" but "Yay parade!" So even today, when something good happens, any one of us might respond with a "Yay parade!" I tell you this only to explain what happened next.

As Christmas drew closer, I began to rethink my decision not to cook. Maybe I could at least cook the greens. Just a few bags of kale, onions, smoked turkey for seasoning (since Omar, Heather's boyfriend did not eat pork), and I'd be done. They probably wouldn't even remember to add a pinch of baking soda anyway. And the macaroni and cheese. No one made macaroni and cheese as good as mine, and Nancy Jean could help by grating the cheese. Well, you can guess how this story ends. I finally had to admit that I did indeed want to cook just as I always had. How to broach the subject to the ladies after setting this whole change in motion could be a problem, but I would put it out there and be willing to go along with the majority as we had always done.

So a group text went out, apologizing for being an indecisive mother and godmother, and asking how they'd feel if I rescinded my decision not to cook and we went back to our usual routine. I quickly received three return texts, each with the same two words: *Yay parade!*

Christmas dinner was wonderful! We had honey-baked ham, honey-baked turkey, stuffing, macaroni and cheese, candied sweet potatoes, and of course, the kale. Rolls and wine rounded out the meal. Dessert consisted of Black Forest cake made by Nancy Jean.

After dinner, I watched as the ladies cleaned up the dining room and kitchen, evenly dividing leftovers and making sure there was enough for Patty, while Esther and I sat by the fireplace. The Christmas music that played during dinner was now replaced by DJ Omar with Prince singing "When Doves Cry." I watched as the girls danced, teased and laughed with each other just as they always had. At that moment, I couldn't imagine why I had thought I wanted to do things differently. Maybe one year things will change, but as I sat watching the familiar scene in the kitchen, all I could think was *Yay parade!*

Nancy McKeever

Flying

The force of the roller coaster caused my eleven-year-old niece Maya and me, as well as the rest of the riders, to pop up in our seats as easily as if we were being manipulated by an invisible puppeteer. We had just finished the first of our double rides on the Pacific Park roller coaster. Maya and I grinned at each other. While Maya had not yet quite been able to mimic me and fling her arms in the air as the cars made their descent at what felt like break-neck speed, she was, in her words, "thinking about it."

"Maya, you don't have to let go of the bar. Just enjoy the ride."

"I know," she said as she smiled in anticipation of the next run.

Amusement parks, and especially riding roller coasters, had been one of the delights of my childhood. In the 1950s, our school picnics were held at Kennywood Park in West Mifflin, a suburb on the outskirts of Pittsburgh. Kennywood was made a national historic landmark in 1987. This park remains open today and some of the original wooden roller coasters are still in use. Although there are more now, when I was eleven years old, there were only four roller coasters in the park if you included the one in Kiddieland. All of these roller-coasters were built in the 1920s. There was The Pippin. Just your run of the mill coaster; not too scary and not too fast, but fun just the same. Next there was The Racer. This consisted of two sets of cars running on tracks that were at times side by side then would veer away from each other only to meet again later down the line. On one stretch of track, the two trains were so close together that you could reach over and slap hands with your friends in the competing cars as you passed. The unquestionable king of the roller coasters was the Jack Rabbit. This coaster consisted of three trains: three cars per train and six seats per car. It was known for its breath-taking seventy-foot drop and its double dip which ejected you out of your seat so forcefully you felt you might fly right off the roller coaster and float over the park waving at all the open-mouthed spectators below. I think that was my secret fantasy; that one day, thanks to the roller coaster, I would be able to fly. The thrill of anticipation as we heard the clacking of the wooden wheels as the cars ascended was followed by the rush of plummeting down those two dips at forty-five miles per hour. It was said that the wheels left the tracks at times, but I don't think I let myself believe that.

  We lived in the Homewood-Brushton area of Pittsburgh and attended the picnic with all the other school children in that district. This included Crescent

Elementary, Baxter Junior High and Westinghouse High School. Everyone we knew attended the picnic and it was a day of family, fun, food and friends. Our mother would fill two huge picnic baskets with fried chicken, potato salad, deviled eggs, Lay's potato chips, fruit and her famous chocolate cake—the same cake we used to sometimes sell to our classmates at lunch time so we could buy a ticket to get a non-homemade dessert from the school cafeteria like the rest of the students. Drinks for the picnic included lemonade, grape Kool-Aid and Faygo red pop.

My mother and her three sisters, Sarah, Clara and Margaret would all board the same bus with the various cousins so we could arrive together and find tables in the same area. The closer we got to the park, the more excited we became. By the time the bus arrived, we were standing at the doors. When the doors opened, we would burst out of the doors like race horses out of the gate with instructions from "the sisters" to "find a good spot with some shade!"

After finding what we were sure was the perfect spot, our mothers would claim our tables by putting the baskets, each covered by a neatly folded tablecloth, in the center of each table. The food would stay there all day, and we could return to the table at any time to grab a bite to eat before returning to the rides. There was never any worry about someone moving your basket or stealing food. It just didn't happen in that seemingly more innocent era. When I was older my mother reminded me that additionally in those days no one worried so much about refrigeration.

"That potato salad and those deviled eggs would sit there all day in the hot summer sun and no one ever got sick after eating it. Why was that?" She said.

I couldn't answer her.

Once arriving at the park, we never ate right away as we were eager to ride. We would start with the tamer rides; Tilt-a-Whirl, The Octopus, The Turtle and The Whip while the aunts took the younger kids to Kiddieland. We were always told to meet back at the tables at five o'clock to ensure that we had one complete meal and could check in with our mothers. I remember returning to the table after an afternoon of rides and plopping down at the first familiar table I came to. It happened to be my Aunt Sarah's table.

She said wickedly and loud enough for all to hear, "Nancy Jean, I don't know what's in your mother's basket but you knew if you came to your Aunt Sarah's table, you'd get some good food."

Without even looking in Aunt Sarah's direction. my mother responded matter of fact, "Well, PeeWee (Sarah's son and my cousin) is skinny as a rail so the boy better come down here and have some of Aunt Susie's chicken and potato salad. Come on PeeWee."

Margaret, the youngest of the sisters chimed in, "I don't know how any of these kids have any meat on their bones 'cause I'm the only one who can really cook!"

Aunt Clara was the last to speak. She was our favorite as she could always be counted on to throw a good swear word around at any time. She ended the conversation by saying, "None of you can cook worth shit so let them kids sit down anywhere and eat!"

The truth was, we could have sat at any table for they all loved us and would have fed us as if we were truly their children. This type of family experience helped to solidify the strong bonds of love that enfolded us always despite the ongoing challenges that poverty presented to us. No one felt poor or 'less than' on Kennywood Day. We were flying!

During dinner, the aunts made their plans for their turn at the rides. The roller coasters were all they rode. Decisions would be made about who would ride when and who would watch the little ones. There was never an argument about this serious subject for everyone wanted to have equal time on the coasters. At the same time, we would be making plans with our cousins to do the same thing. After dinner, a short rest and repeated pleas of,

"Can we go now?" we would be off to ride as much as possible before the day ended. We would warm up on the Pippin, crowding into the seats as if this would be the last chance ever to enjoy the ride. On the Racer it would be boys against girls, cousins against cousins, or just a free for all with any of us sitting anywhere; slapping hands whenever the cars were in close enough proximity to give us an opportunity to do so. On the fearsome Jackrabbit, there was always a skirmish for the very first seat which was thought to be the most dangerous. The boys always won but at times would give up their seat to a girl cousin or sister for "just one ride!"

We would ride the coasters until it was time to meet at the tables one last time, pack everything up, leave the park and board the bus back to Homewood, each year declaring that this was the best school picnic ever.

I was brought back to the present by Maya softly tapping my arm and asking that I hold her phone for the final ride. I didn't ask, but I knew that she was trying to decide on whether to throw her hands up in the air. Putting her phone deep in my pocket, we exchanged conspiratorial grins, placed our hands on the bar and readied ourselves to fly.

The Gifts of Music

I can't recall who said it,
I know I've never read it,
I only know they tell me that love is grand,
And....

That's the song that's in my head when I awaken today. I often wake up with a melody in my head, not always an old standard; it could be anything from a few measures of the "Flower Duet" from Lakmé or parts of *The Pearl Fishers* to something by Roberta Flack or my favorite, Frank Sinatra. Music has always been an integral part of my life. The gift of music opened up a whole new world for me, one in which I often felt transported to another place and time, where I was introduced to a source of beauty that I had not known existed before. I remember when I was seven and our only source of music was a small plastic-covered radio that sat in a place of honor on top of our icebox. In the morning hours it would be tuned to what we called the "old folks' station." This meant that we would hear "Near You" by the Andrews Sisters or "Time After Time" by Frank Sinatra. In the afternoon, however, the radio belonged to us. It was then that we listened to what was initially called Black music and later called rhythm and blues. Our favorite program was hosted by a disc jockey named Porky Chedwick. He opened the show by boasting, "This is W-A-M-O, WAMO!! And I'm Porky Chedwick, your platter pushin' papa, your Daddio of the Raddio!!! Yeah, I'm the Bossman playin' oldies but goodies and some new stuff too for all you movers and groovers!!"

We thought he was very cool, especially for a white man. Porky played our music, "Sixty Minute Man" by Fats Domino and "Take Me Back Baby" by Count Basie, music that allowed us to sing and dance around that small apartment as if we were in a grand ballroom. This was my first experience enjoying music, but it wasn't long before I found out that making music was just as enjoyable as listening to it. I was in the fourth grade and had the chance to take a music class. Students with excellent grades were given the opportunity to choose an instrument to learn. By the time it was my turn to choose an instrument, only the B-flat clarinet remained. I played the clarinet in both the orchestra and the marching band through twelfth grade. I absolutely loved it! I played classical orchestra music during the week and executed marching band formations at football games on Friday nights—the best of both worlds!

Westinghouse High School was famous for its

football team made up of the sons of steelworkers and other blue-collar workers. We won the city high school football championship almost every year and had a trophy case full of trophies to prove it. But it was through my orchestra experience that I was introduced to and learned to love classical music. Our teacher in both junior high and high school was Mr. Carl McVicker, a tall, thin gentle soul with reddish brown hair and a bushy reddish-brown mustache. Mr. McVicker loved music and used to cry when we interpreted a piece of music correctly. He helped us learn to love and appreciate the classics.

My most memorable orchestra experience occurred when I was in the eleventh grade. Every year there was a contest between the high school orchestras. The top four high schools to play in this contest were Alderdice, Mount Lebanon, Schenley, and Westinghouse. Every year Mount Lebanon came in first and Westinghouse second. We, of course, thought they had an unfair advantage, as their student body was mostly comprised of Jewish students with upper-class, well-to-do parents who could afford private lessons for their children after first buying them their own instruments. They had no need to wait around for a turn to sign out and borrow an instrument from school to practice on at home as we less fortunate students often did. We thought surely we could have won if only we had had these same advantages, but truthfully perhaps this was just salve for our wounds of not winning year after year. This particular year, when the winners were announced, this is what we heard: "Third place, Alderdice High School; second place, Mount Lebanon High School; and first place, Westinghouse High School."

Since it was considered unprofessional to show any signs of jubilance when the winner was announced, we had to sit quietly at "parade rest" until all the orchestras filed out of the auditorium in alphabetical order. The other orchestra members and I sat with our backs straight, me with my clarinet resting on my right knee, the mouthpiece pointing straight up to the sky...waiting... waiting. As soon as the auditorium was empty except for the judges, Mr. McVicker, tears streaming down his face, tossed his baton into the air and was immediately engulfed in a swarm of cheering, crying students, hugging and clapping. Finally, we had won first place! In the next day's *Pittsburgh Post-Gazette*, the headline read "Westinghouse has two champions now." Our trophy was placed in the showcase along with all the football trophies.

I stopped playing the clarinet after high school but obtained most of my fill of music while in nursing school by watching *American Bandstand*. After my classmates and I finished our clinical rotation each day, we would rush to the dorms as quickly as we could, remove our starched white aprons, and gather in the lounge to catch up on all the latest music and dances. It's only now that I reflect on the fact that there were no African American faces among the *American Bandstand* participants. In the early '60s African American dancers were not welcome on the show although African American performers were. I didn't think much of it at the time and just accepted that this was the way it was. So along with my white classmates, I sang along with "Take Good Care of My Baby" and danced to "The Bristol Stomp," waiting for another door that remained closed to us to open. We would have to wait until 1970, when *Soul Train*, a predominantly African American dance program with a format much like American Bandstand, was aired before we saw ourselves reflected both in the performers and in the audience.

After nursing school came marriage, children, and eventually a marital separation. Wanting my children to have a taste of something other than their pop music (although I listened to that also), and after seeing the play with a music enthusiast, Esther and I took the girls to see Evita with Patti LuPone and Mandy Patinkin. Unsure about they would react to the play, especially the youngest one, who was nine, I made sure that they understood this was unlike anything they had experienced before but hoped they would enjoy the music and action of the story.

My Mother's Daughter

I had no reason to worry. They were enthralled with the play and begged to see it again. Giving in to their pleas, we took them a second time. Today, they each still have a copy of the *Evita* CD and can be heard singing snippets of the songs with surprising regularity.

Music is also often in the background when I'm cooking. I usually start off with someone like Adele—nice and easy, melodic, sing-along tunes. When I need a little more energetic stimulus, it's Lady Gaga for a vibrant and toe-tapping beat. For something requiring the maximum effort, like hours of long preparation for Thanksgiving dinner, I crank up the all-stops-out music of Prince and a song like "Baby I'm a Star." This is music where you have to keep yourself from dancing so you can mix up that sweet potato pie to its pulsing rhythms. It makes cooking much more fun!

One of the only times I don't listen to music is when I write. I find it unnecessary and intrusive, as to me writing has its own rhythm, its own melody, its own tempo, and its own phrasing. I write in silence.

So, as you can see, music is with me most of the day. My evenings are spent watching my favorite TV shows or a good movie. And yet, when the TV goes off, I end my day in the same way it started. I immediately turn on my CD player and receive one final gift from music as it lulls me to sleep:

Nancy McKeever

The thing that's known as romance
 Is wonderful, wonderful
 In every way, so they say.

A Gentle Touch of Memory

I looked closely at my right hand. I had never really paid attention to any aspect of my hand in the past, but today I paused and paid closer attention to the details. I was completing the everyday task of brushing my teeth, and as I went to scoop up water to rinse, it registered that I was holding my hand exactly the way I remember my mother holding her hand at times. I studied it for a few seconds, noting how the little finger lay comfortably beside the finger next to it, with the rest of the fingers all following in line, except for the thumb, which lay lazily off to one side. On second thought, maybe my hands didn't really look like my mother's. Now I'm not sure. Maybe they just make me think of her and her hands.

With the life she lived, you would expect my mother's hands to have been chafed, rough, and calloused. After all, these were the same hands that scrubbed other people's floors as well as her own. For other people, hopefully, she had a mop. But her own floor was done with her down on her hands and knees with a scrub bucket and a rag, usually an old piece of towel. The cracked linoleum floor in our tenement apartment was white with small black dots on it. Peering closely at the floor, she made sure she didn't miss an odd piece of food that had escaped her brisk broom, which had swept the floor a few minutes before.

"I don't want to leave the roaches any dinner," she would say. "They'll come anyway, but I don't want to welcome them!" She would scrub every inch of that floor, let it dry, and then wax it. In those days, she had to use wax that took a little time to dry. Each and every time before waxing, she would say to us, "Get what you need from the kitchen because my waxed floor will take a while to dry."

Inevitably, while the waxed floor was drying, one of us would say, "Momma, I forgot my pencil/book/paper. If I walk around the edges, can I just go in and get it real fast?"

She wouldn't answer. She would just give the speaker a look; the same look she gave us in church if we were giggling or not paying attention. The look that meant NO and there was no further discussion!

Another chore for those hands was laundry. Not having a washer and dryer, all laundry was done by hand. Using two large metal tubs, a washboard, a bar of soap, and plenty of elbow grease, my mother had to also take on this arduous task. She'd get the garment wet, soap it up while it was up against the rippled washboard, and scrub energetically until the article in question was clean. Once sufficiently wrung out from the soapy water, it was plunged into the rinse water, sometimes twice, wrung out again, and then placed in a large basket until it could be hung on the line to dry.

Washing my father's work clothes was an important part of wash day, as they were a crucial contribution to maintaining his daily safety. Two sets of long underwear were used as protection against the burning embers that occasionally flew from the open hearth furnace. Part of his job as a steelworker was to get close enough to the furnace to enable him to "feed" it with a shovel. The burns on his back attested to the fact that this was not quite enough protection. When questioned about it, he would dismiss it as one of the unavoidable aspects of his job.

I was concerned about my mother's risk of injury also.

"Does that hurt your hand, Momma?" I asked one day while she was doing laundry.

"No, baby. You hold the clothes so that they act as a cushion against the washboard. When you don't hold it the right way, yes, it can hurt."

When I was a little older and helping out by washing small pieces of clothing, I found out exactly what she meant. We started helping at a young age by first filling the tubs, getting a fresh bar of soap, and then gathering the clothespins so we could hand them to my mother as she worked her way down the clothesline.

Most times she hung the clothes outside, but when it rained, or in the winter, the clothes were hung inside on lines strung across the kitchen. This meant navigating your way carefully around the kitchen, bending deeply to avoid being slapped in the face by a wet sock or worse yet, a pair of jeans. I loved when she hung the clothes outside, especially on a hot windy day, loved the feel of the sheets billowing against my face and dancing with me when buffeted by the wind. But I was careful not to let my mother see me dancing with her clean sheets. Or it was "Nancy, don't wipe your sweaty face against my clean sheets! I'm not washing them again! And don't get that head wet!! I'm not sweating over a hot stove for that hair until next weekend!"

What I thought was fun when I was young became a source of embarrassment when I was a little older, and I lived in fear that a classmate would see me wrestling with those clothes on the line. I used to try and bury my head in the wet clothes as I hung them, hoping no one would see me, for continuing to hang clothes outside long after most others had stopped let everyone know how little we had. Even in this poor community, we were still among the poorest of the poor.

Straightening my hair, and that of my sisters, was another chore for those hands. Small burns from either the hot comb or the open flame on the stove were not uncommon. We sisters were not the most cooperative on hair days, dawdling in order to prevent the start of the procedure or not sitting still on the little purple stool used for that purpose. I didn't appreciate my mother's patience until I had daughters of my own. Reluctant to wrestle with my first daughter's hair, I only combed it superficially until it became a knotted mess. In tears one day, I took her to my mother, who after much tsking and a stern lecture on what I hadn't done, should do, and had better do in the future, she combed my daughter's hair for what she made clear was the first and last time. She even gave me a straightening comb, which I have kept all these many years. A clear reminder of a lesson learned the hard way.

    I have to add some additional information about the floor scrubbing as the opening description does not quite cover all the perils inherent in scrubbing an old kitchen floor. Our floor had some areas that were so old and cracked that they allowed both large and small pieces of unrecognizable debris to collect in the cracks. That meant we had to first dig out what was in the crack and then proceed to scrub the area clean. I remember on one occasion my mother was cleaning out an area around a kitchen pipe. She was repeatedly pulling on a "string," which when she finally retrieved it, she found out it was the tail of a mouse with the body of the mouse still attached! That was one time when the task of finishing the scrubbing of the floor was delegated to Chuckie!

Last, but certainly not least, of the chores for these revered hands was the project of canning. Momma and two of her sisters would crowd into our small kitchen. We would be there also, only on the periphery, as our job was to dispose of the unusable fruit usually found at the very bottom of the huge baskets, while also avoiding the boiling pots of water that bubbled on every burner of the stove. This process was always done in the heat of a Pittsburgh summer, but the canned goods would be used mostly in the winter. It was in the winter that my father's steelworkers' union would often go on strike so he had no work, and only got paid for the four hours a day that he walked the picket line. Scarce money would mean scarce food, and my mother knew she would have to be creative by adding the tomatoes to an otherwise dull dinner of lima beans or using the peaches as a substitute for jelly or maybe a dessert for a little something sweet in the evening.

I would watch as my mother and her sisters bent perilously over the steaming pots in the sweltering kitchen. They would dip the fruit into the hot water with their bare hands. This loosened the skin on the fruit so that it was easier to peel. Initially, I was afraid that someday they would misjudge the heat of the steaming liquid, dip their hands into the hot water, and both the fruit and their fingers would come out of the water with skin hanging loosely, scalded by the hot liquid. Of course, this never happened, and we continued to enjoy the literal fruits of their labor.

So many chores over so many years, and yet today I am questioning how my mother's hands looked. I have never doubted how they felt. What I remember without question are two hands softly cupping my face followed by a gentle kiss on the forehead. This was my mother's greeting each time I went to visit, whether I was visiting from Pittsburgh or Los Angeles. It was always the same.

"Hello, sweetie," she would say, and no matter what was going on in my life, I felt soothed.

Nancy McKeever

My Mother's Daughter

SPEAKING OF RACE

Like a Fly in Buttermilk

"Like a fly in buttermilk." How many times had I heard that phrase and why was I thinking of it now? It didn't take long to figure out. I was thinking about the new writing class I'd registered for at Emeritus College. I found myself automatically considering what the ethnic composition of the class might be, revisiting the age-old question of whether or not there would be other Black participants.

"Like a fly in buttermilk" refers to a Black person being in a situation where they are the only dark person in a sea of white or non-Black faces. I tried to remember the first time I had heard those words. I think it was when I was in the fourth grade. A note was sent home stating that I had done exceptionally well on some now forgotten test, and for that reason and with my parents' permission, I could skip a grade and be placed in a special class. I heard my mother discussing it with her sister Clara.

"It sounds good, Clara. This program is one day a week, and the letter says the classes are at a higher level. What's even better is that they serve the students lunch. One less lunch to worry about one day of the week. It's only a little bit of money but even a little bit helps."

"It does sound good, Susie, and who knows where

it can lead? She might be the only fly in the buttermilk, but one is better than none."

What does that mean? Is it good or bad? I wondered. "Momma," I asked later, "what did Aunt Clara mean about the fly in the buttermilk?"

"Baby, she was only saying that you might be the only Black student in this class, but this is a good opportunity. You were picked because they see how smart you are, and we need to take advantage of every chance we can get."

While I know that my mother was trying in her own way to protect and prepare me, it caused me to approach the class with some trepidation. You must remember this was in the early 1950s, and racial issues were just as complex then as they are today. Even though many important events for African Americans occurred in the '50s, racism was alive and well in Pittsburgh and being Black still required a high level of hypervigilance in every situation. Racism was/is like an insidious gas that taints the very fabric of your life. I have wondered, if in trying to protect us, my mother only served to inflame an already highly sensitive issue. But sadly, I have learned that this was not true. She did what she needed to do at the time to protect her children in the only way she knew.

Entrance into and participation in the writing class went without incident, and I enjoyed it and made many friends. This scenario, however, repeated itself at other times in my life. I thought of it when I was one of only two Black students in my nursing school class. When assigned a "big sister," as we all were, I noted that there were only two Black students in the class ahead of us. Was there a quota or was this just a coincidence? I'll never know. Even when I completed training, was gainfully employed, and rose through the ranks, there were initially very few Black charge nurses or unit supervisors and even fewer Black nursing directors. So, in many administrative meetings, I was still "a fly in buttermilk." This, of course, changed fairly quickly over the years, but I still carried the thought deep or maybe not so deep within me. Not that I thought of it constantly, but it remained dormant in my subconscious like a sleeping poisonous snake that could be easily awakened by a situation such as registering for a new class. Racism and the effects of racism are far-reaching and at times crippling to an individual.

Despite all of this, I believe my life and that of my two daughters has gone well. I thought of them when this question arose for me and realized that I had no idea if they felt the same way. We had always talked about racial issues and dealt with its effects. I remember my eight-year-old daughter coming home upset and angry because a classmate accused her of "talking too white." "I talk the way we always talk," she declared angrily.

"Yes, you do," I responded "and there is no reason for you to change. Perhaps this girl needs to listen and learn from you." That's when you realize that you have to teach your children that there are many facets of racism. Not just white against Black but Black against Black, brown against yellow, and a whole spectrum of prejudicial ideologies.

So I asked my daughters, ages fifty-two and forty-seven at the time, if they experienced the "fly in buttermilk" question when they approached new situations.

My younger daughter Nancy Jean has Tourette's syndrome, which is a neurological syndrome characterized by physical and verbal tics that are very noticeable and have made her life extremely difficult. Her social life is less full than her sister's, but she is outgoing and personable and I think her Tourette's makes her work harder at creating a favorable impression on others. She had many friends of all races when she was in school, after a period of education of both students and teachers.

"No, I don't usually automatically think about that," she said. "I'm usually more worried about other things like my Tourette's when I'm using public transportation, etc. Sometimes people stare at me or laugh, and that doesn't feel good. The only time I did think about it was when I was invited to a friend's wedding whose husband was part of a motorcycle club, and I had visions of *Sons of Anarchy* behavior going on. But that was more MY fear than actual danger, and I had no problems."

Stacey, my older daughter, has a much more eclectic social life and has friends from diverse races. She earned a master's degree in Library and Information Sciences from UCLA and works as a manager of digital asset management. Stacey attends the Hollywood Bowl on a regular basis, and loves Trivia Night, which is held at the bar down the street from her home; her racially diverse team has taken first prize several times. She volunteers for KCRW and has attempted to be part of a group held at the downtown L.A. public library that read (I think) *The Odyssey* over one weekend. She's always busy doing interesting things. She answered my same question without hesitation. "Depends on where I'm going, but yep, that's always in the back of my mind. Especially if I'm going somewhere where I feel white people act surprised like, oh, do Black folks like this too? It never stops me though. I go where I want to go."

Both answers made me exquisitely sad, as each of them did indeed have their own burden to carry in this life.

Nancy McKeever

The Color of Friendship

"I've never seen anyone with so many visitors," Alexa, my nurse for the day, said as she entered my hospital room. The current visitors, in various stages of departure, were my sister Mimsi, brother-in-law Robert, daughter Nancy Jean, goddaughter Heather, my deceased best friend's wife Carolynn, and a fellow nurse friend who worked there at Saint John's. Her name was Sudie, and she had run in, as had many others, on her fifteen-minute break, just to say hello. I had worked at Saint John's some years ago as director of the inpatient psychiatric program until the program was closed after the destruction and remodeling brought on by the 1994 Northridge earthquake. Although some psychiatric staff had left with the closing of the Ross Psychiatric Center, many had stayed and moved to different departments within the hospital. The hospital grapevine had let them know I was there. Following close behind Alexa was my surgeon, Dr. McKenna, and his office manager (and wife) Kathy.

After a flurry of goodbye hugs and kisses from my visitors, the doctor and I were able to discuss my progress, which included the possibility of discharge the next day.

"Too bad you don't have more of a support system,"

he joked as he left the room.

It wasn't until I was home and recuperating that I connected that incident with an exchange I had had years earlier with my then-therapist. I had been considering writing about that conversation for some time, and for some reason, the visitor situation triggered it in my mind again. For reasons still not quite clear to me, I could not formulate exactly what I wanted to say, how I wanted to say it, or even why. I also couldn't remember how the patient/therapist question was resolved. However, I felt it needed to be shared. Maybe if I just started writing, these questions would be answered.

I cannot recall the context in which the conversation with my therapist occurred. I just remember her statement, not verbatim, but here's the gist of it.

"Nancy, you must realize that most of your friends are white. Have you thought about the fact that you have so many non-Black friends?"

My initial reaction was a mixture of anger and guilt. I knew enough to know that in the psychological world, a strong reaction such as mine usually meant one of two things. Either the statement was true or actually untrue and the therapist had totally missed the patient. My first thought was what right did this white woman, fifteen years younger than me, have to be questioning me about my friendships in such an accusatory manner?

In retrospect, I must admit that I don't really know if it was accusatory or if I just heard it that way. I am sure about the feelings of guilt. I immediately began questioning myself about my friends. Yes, there was diversity, but how much and was it enough? And who was to say how much was enough?

What can one say about a society where being raised poor and Black in the 1940s and '50s left you still doubting everything about yourself because of your race? There have always been racial complications even within the Black community itself. When I was a young girl in the 1950s, Black Power was not yet a full-grown movement, but there were implications centered around skin tone and the depth of your Blackness in the Black community. Being the lightest-skinned of my siblings, I was often teased or tormented for not being Black enough. As if somehow being darker made you more innately Black than someone with a lighter skin color. There used to be a rhyme that kids would repeat that went like this:

If you're white, you're alright,
If you're brown, stick around,
But if you're Black, get w-a-a-a-ay back.

For someone like me, who at that time was very light-skinned with reddish brown hair, I would often be a target of ridicule, even from my own siblings when I did something to displease them. It was only when I was older (and darker) that I understood that this came from years of both subtle and overt racism both inside and outside the Black community, where lightness gave you superiority and could therefore be a source of envy, where even I found myself admiring the lighter-skinned friend with less kinky hair. I remember a stand-up comedy bit by Whoopi Goldberg in which she pretended to be a white girl. She would drape a large yellow towel over her head to denote blonde hair and talk in a Valley Girl voice, flicking her towel of hair back over her shoulders at intervals. Blacks and non-Blacks used to laugh at this bit, and my sisters and I used to take turns using the yellow towel, but what was that really saying about us as young Black women pretending to be white? I didn't question that, or many other things, until I was older and wiser.

Growing up, I lived in a neighborhood that was a mixture of Italian and Black. Everyone seemed to get along, but even in that outwardly accepting neighborhood, we were taught that you could not really trust white people. It didn't matter how nice they appeared to be; you were never to forget that they considered themselves superior to you and would be quick to remind you of that if necessary. I didn't want to believe that, but when you're told something often enough in so many ways, how can you not believe? My mother, who often quoted the Golden Rule—"Do unto others as you would have them do unto you"—cleaned other people's homes for a living, all of whom treated her well. One woman used to fix lunch for both of them and they would eat lunch together every week on my mother's cleaning day and sit and talk like two friends. Yet one week this woman overpaid my mother by a dollar. My mother only discovered this after walking five blocks in the hot, humid Pittsburgh summer sun to her bus stop. As she told me later, she thought that maybe her employer was "testing" her, so she walked those sizzling five blocks back to the house to return the dollar. The woman apologized for my mother's having to retrace her route home and told her to keep the extra dollar. This is only one sad example of the burden of paranoia under which my mother and many Blacks lived every day.

Throughout school, I attended predominantly Black but racially mixed schools. I did have Black best friends during these years but also my share of non-Black friends. This only changed when I entered nurses training. Receiving a scholarship from the Jewish Women's Auxiliary League of Montefiore Hospital allowed me to attend nurses school tuition-free, the only way I could have furthered my education. The environment here was very different. Out of approximately 100 students in various stages of their nursing careers, I was one of seven Black students. I must admit to some initial anxiety, but at no point did I ever feel any discrimination from my classmates. We were all in the same situation: new, eager to learn, and scared to death we were going to kill someone. I had a few racial incidents with patients during training but was always fully supported by my classmates, upperclassmen, and clinical instructors. I loved training and made close friends, some of whom I am still in contact with via Facebook.

After graduation, the situation was much the same. I was an excellent nurse and had the skill of team building, which was recognized and rewarded. I moved quickly up the administrative ladder, which at this time remained mostly white. I would, on occasion, notice that I was the only Black director in the room, but I was doing my job, doing it well, and enjoying my colleagues with no thought to the composition of my social circle.

But perhaps my therapist's question reminded me of those incidents when I envied those who did not carry the burden of Blackness, those who could move through the world easily, never worrying about being judged upon sight before you even had a chance to let the world know who you were, what you thought, or your hopes and dreams. Those who never felt the pressure of having to be better than everyone else in every way. Maybe I never answered my therapist's questions because I needed more time to find the answers. I had to be willing to admit to my own envy and my own prejudice. I believe we all have some prejudice buried deep or maybe not so deep inside us.

I have come to realize many things over the years and have more readily accepted both my attributes and my flaws. Hopefully, in some ways I have changed for the better. Some things remain the same. I continue to make friends easily and enjoy all that I gain from the diversity of my social circle. I enjoy my activities and feel blessed when I review the current list of all my old and newer friends and realize they are all similar. They are all kind, intelligent, gracious, supportive, funny, and generous of spirit. I would not hesitate to call on any of them.

Believe

For months I have felt like Atlas, carrying a burden no one should have to bear. This emotional and physical state was triggered by the outpouring of anger and grief and the multitude of demonstrations surrounding George Floyd's death. His death, and the subsequent events, set in motion for me personally a period of time in which I lived a schizophrenic type of existence. I am fairly sure that outwardly I appeared to have the same reaction as many other people: distressed by the repeated television images and the obvious injustice of the situation. However, inside I was a seething cauldron of anger and bitterness and grief and shame. Certainly, I was no stranger to racism. I've been called the N-word, purposely passed over in a store while a white person was waited on before me, been humiliated about the texture of my hair, and other incidents too numerous to count.

But my mother always taught us to act as if these things didn't bother us. She wanted us to behave as if we were protected against every hurtful act by some protective "Black mother shield," something that would not allow any vile comments or events to affect us. It was rather like "the talk" that some Black fathers have with their sons. But Black mothers automatically cover all their children. And that's what she did; she covered us with her shield of love and kept us walking proudly, head held high, not giving the slightest indication that anything negative truly impacted us. She would repeatedly tell us, "Someone might have more money than you, they might have nicer clothes than you, they might live in a bigger house than you, but NO ONE is better than you!"

But of course, in reality, the shield was not always effective, as we really weren't impervious to these slights, and while I may not have reacted to them, I still carried the knowledge that the burden of this inequity was never far away. Once, as a ten-year-old, I was playing tag in the playground and was tagged by a playmate. She tapped me lightly on the shoulder and said "Gotcha, porch monkey!" Now really, I don't believe I had ever heard that particular phrase before, but somehow I knew it was not good. Filled with a sudden blinding rage, I ran after her and slapped her so hard on her stomach that I left my handprint on her abdomen. Looking on in horror as she vomited on the ground, I was appalled by what I had done, terrified by the intensity of my rage. I was banned from the playground for two weeks and went home crying to my mother.

"She shouldn't have called you names, but I told you, you never know when something like this will happen, and it WILL happen again. You can't let them see that it touches you! I wish I could have slapped her myself, but I would have ended up in jail!"

Never again did I allow my anger to show outwardly in such an obvious way. Not as a nursing student when a patient was allowed to refuse to let me care for her, not when I went to the local White Castle with my nursing school classmates and a little boy innocently asked his mother why my skin was so dirty, not even when the school itself broke its tradition of featuring a picture of the graduating class president in the *Pittsburgh Post-Gazette* but made me, the first Black president, share the honor with a white classmate and close friend because it "looked better." In my early days as a nursing administrator, I learned to deal with a client's surprise when they demanded to "see the supervisor" and could not hide their shock upon seeing me. Of course, by that time, I had learned that the right words could have a stronger effect than a slap on the abdomen, and I had learned to use my words well. There were a multitude of unexpected incidents where I couldn't or didn't react but instead pulled that shield tighter around my battered psyche.

So, life went on with me living happily with my family and my very diverse group of friends. knowing that racism was out there as always but that I would continue, as always, to live with it. And then they killed George Floyd—as they had killed so many others before him. Killed him like a dog in the street, like he was just another piece of trash in that gutter. What finally pushed me over the edge, after watching the video over and over, each time promising myself this would be the very last time, was when they published that in his last breath, he called for his mother.

"Momma," he said.

Was he calling out for her help? Did he actually think he saw her standing there with her Black Momma shield waiting to take him away from the hatred and humiliation and pain?

I don't know, but what it incited in me was to start on a frenzied search for every horrible incident involving Black people that I could find. I wanted to know about the history that had not been printed in history books, and never taught to me nor to my daughters. I was astounded at what I found and ashamed of what I did not know. I knew, for example, about surgery performed without anesthesia on Black patients, Black men given syphilis and deliberately left untreated, the treatment of Jackie Robinson, Emmett Till, Rosa Parks, and Ruby Bridges, all the way up to and including Breonna Taylor. But other incidents, unknown to me, were uncovered in my feverish search for horrific incidents, which, because they were unknown to me, made me feel even worse. The burning of homes and killing of residents in a well-to-do

Black town referred to as the Black Wall Street in Tulsa, Oklahoma, in 1921 was horrible. Even more horrible, the padlocking of the Arkansas Negro Boys Industrial School in Wrightsville, Arkansas, in 1959. One night the school doors were padlocked, and the school was then set on fire. Only forty-eight of sixty-nine boys were able to claw their way to safety; the other twenty-one boys burned to death. Did they too call out in despair for their Mommas? I was seventeen in 1959—why hadn't I read about this in one of the two Black magazines of that time—*Jet* or *Ebony*? I felt I should have known!

  This is the kind of obsessive thinking that filled my days and haunted my sleep until I finally recognized how unhealthy this was for me. I couldn't change it, and I had to stop picking at this bleeding wound hoping that if I caused myself enough pain, I would somehow feel less guilty about my ignorance and thus feel better in some way. It didn't work. And so, I started to talk about it to others, to my family, my wife, my friends of all ages and races. I learned that in every race there is guilt, hatred, shame, regret, and yes, indifference. I learned that there were people out there who, like me, wanted a change, even if we didn't or couldn't march and dance in the street like all those young people of every color, shape, and gender that we saw protesting on TV. I talked, and I listened, not always agreeing, but listening anyway.

I am better now, not great, but certainly not the frenzied wreck I had been. I am mostly sad for all people of all races who have suffered, continue to suffer, and will continue to suffer until we as a country come together.

I must believe the racial, economic, and ecological chaos currently smothering our country can be addressed if we all work together toward healing. I must believe I can cling tightly to these current feelings of hope. I must believe that George Floyd did indeed see his Momma as he died.

Jackassery

Jackassery. My favorite new word. The word used by Republican U.S. Senator Ben Sasse when describing the antics of some of his colleagues during the confirmation hearings of Judge Ketanji Brown Jackson. He used that word because these "gentleman" took this opportunity to make blatant accusations and criticisms masking as political sound bites rather than using the time as intended, which was to make an honest assessment of Judge Jackson's qualifications to sit on the Supreme Court of the United States. Democratic Senator Cory Booker responded to this behavior by delineating specifically the countless intricate steps it took for Judge Jackson or any other minority female to attain a place of prominence in this racist, sexist, and misogynistic world. I use it now to describe any micro- or macro-aggressive act toward another of any disparate gender or race.

I watched much of these proceedings with anger and disgust but also with pride as Judge Jackson handled herself with aplomb throughout the proceedings. I knew from being a minority woman, although in no way on Judge Brown's level, some of what she must have gone through to arrive where she is today. To survive this, I know she must have had ongoing strong encouragement and support from both friends and family, especially from her mother, who as another Black female, must have experienced some form of jackassery from a very young age and throughout her life, just as I did.

Here are two examples of jackassery in two different stages of my life.

"Mommy, look! That girl's skin is all brown. Is she dirty? She's not white like us. Look, Mommy!"

This from a young white boy to his very embarrassed mother as we stood in the checkout line in the Thoroughfare Super Market in Pittsburgh in 1949. I was young, young enough to become tearful at these harsh words, but I was old enough to know that this was a hurtful experience having to do with being a Black person in a very white world. I buried my face in my mother's sturdy thigh and clung to her, wishing I could climb back into the safe warmth of her womb. She, in turn, gently cupped my face in her hands, raised my face to look at hers, kissed me on my forehead, and said, "It's all right sweetie. He's not a very smart boy or else he would remember that every summer many white people pour on sunscreen and lie in the sun for hours so they can be just as brown as you are now. Do you remember that?"

Of course I did. And so, I was able to pull myself together and face the horrible situation head-on. I imagined that my mother watched this transformation with both anger and pride. I also remember two additional maxims that she repeated many times in my life. First, she reminded me: "Words are just that, words, and saying them does not make them true." Regardless of how I felt, she wanted me to try to give the appearance of strength, to soldier on, head held high, wrapped in the impenetrable shield of her love. The second catchphrase was "Never let them see you cry." Don't ever let your enemies realize that those words you were so desperately trying to ignore had actually found their mark. At that moment, I felt better thanks to my mother's explanation, but as I grew older, I realized that there would be times when I would have to remind myself that, yes, I was at least good enough and at times even better. But no matter the age or circumstances, the threat of being looked down upon and thought of as less capable or less deserving was never far away and could appear at any time to shatter my self-confidence and dreams.

    I would need to recall my mother's words at other times in my life. Another example of the need for motherly repair occurred when I was much older and in my first year of nursing school. As first-year students, we were assigned only one patient for whom we rendered care. These patients were labeled "completes," which meant that everything had to be done for them. They needed assistance brushing their teeth, eating, washing their hair, and bathing, after which their bed had to be changed, medications dispensed, and their room left neat and clean. The patient I was assigned to was blind and had difficulty hearing, so communication with her was difficult. I did manage to complete what I thought was an excellent job of meeting her every need and was finally ready to leave her room when I heard her say, "I'm glad you took care of me today instead of one of those niggers. They are so rough and mean, and you know they even smell funny."

Shocked, I could think of no response. Instead of feeling like a professional nurse who had just done a good job, once again I was that young girl whose feelings were hurt and whose vision was blurred by tears. My supervisor, a Black woman herself who had overheard the insult, ordered me not to cry and to keep on with my work.

I completed my charting, went directly to the dorms, shut myself in the phone booth, and called my mother. As soon as I heard her warm, soothing voice, the dam burst, and I sobbed out my story. How difficult the patient was, what a thorough job I had done, her last words to me, and Miss Wilkins' reaction. She let me finish and encouraged me to cry for as long as I needed to.

"You can always cry with Momma, sweetie. You did a great job with that mean old woman. She is very unhappy and probably has been unhappy about something most of her life, but you will never be like her. You have more than she has right now, and you are just getting started. She will never be more than she is now. And she will never know that she made you cry."

Once again, an example of pride and anger standing side by side. Once again, my mother had helped to ease my pain. Not that she could erase what had happened, but her love was a buffer against the realities of life. And it helped to solidify the idea that I could go on from incidents such as this and know in my heart that, yes, I was more than good enough.

I continued to discuss incidents of all kinds with my mother throughout my life. Not because I was looking for advice about my professional duties. I was a nurse administrator, and my mother had cleaned houses for a living. While she was not familiar with hospital policy and administration, she was a magician when it came to people and human nature. Discussions with her helped me to clarify the important points of my concerns, solidify my thoughts, and regain my composure at that time. I retired proud of my accomplishments and well respected in my chosen field of inpatient and outpatient psychiatry, thanks in large part to her unflagging encouragement and support.

Ketanji Brown Jackson's confirmation was arduous and challenging. But she was poised, professional, and patient throughout all the inane jackassery. She, like me, had many supporters all her life who reminded her of how very special she was, who taught her how to walk through this world proving her supporters were right, and that she was more than just good enough. Just as I thank my mother for all she gave me, Judge Brown stood in the gallery and thanked all her supporters. She gave a special thank you to "the woman whom I love most in this world...my mother." And while I was not in that gallery to hear this proclamation, I am sure that pride and anger were once again there standing shoulder to shoulder.

My Mother's Daughter

Susie and Nancy

Susie

Susie

GOODBYE SUE

Before I'm Gone

I try to imagine two young girls walking along a dusty country road. They are approximately eleven and thirteen years old and similar in build, with the older of the two just a little heavier than her sister. Two pairs of long, skinny legs can be seen poking out from underneath their plain cotton dresses. Puffs of dust mark their progress as their bare feet kick up dirt and sometimes other less welcome debris.

"Damn, cow shit on my feet!" says Clara, the elder, and our favorite aunt. She started cursing at a young age and would continue to do so all her life, much to the delight of her six nieces and nephews.

"I hate it too!" says her younger sister Susie (my mother) who, unlike her favorite sister, seldom curses, much to her children's disappointment. "Why is it always us?" Susie grumbles. "It's always 'Susie and Clara, go get the cows.' What's wrong with Emma or Sarah or even baby Margaret? She's eight and needs to start learning. We can't do it forever!"

They make their way home as they do every evening, bonded even more solidly by their mutual agreement that they are being treated unfairly. These two sisters remain very close all their lives, speak daily by phone, commiserate on raising children while in the depths of poverty, and bemoan the infidelity of their respective husbands. They see each other weekly at Friday night Pokeno, which is also attended by their other sisters, Emma, Sarah and "baby" Margaret, well into their 70s.

I can only imagine most of this conversation from pieces of information gleaned from my mother during my yearly October visit to Pittsburgh. It was my favorite trip, as I had my mother mostly to myself. I loved the fall with the leaves changing colors, the fallen ones crunching noisily under my feet like a huge bag of potato chips.

So again, why must I imagine? After spending so much uninterrupted time with my mother, why am I now at this point in my life examining all the unasked and therefore unanswered questions about my mother's life? How did this young girl raised on a farm in the borough of Wilkinsburg in Pittsburgh become the woman she was? A woman who lost her mother at an early age, although the exact age of my grandmother when she died is one of my unasked questions. A woman who successfully raised six children mostly on her own. I know she and her sisters were sent to live with their mother's sister, who was also named Sue. My mother described her Aunt Sue as a mean person who jeered at her voracious thirst for reading. But she obviously read, and read a lot. How else could she open our bedroom door with my two sisters and me in various states of undress getting ready for school, and smilingly say, "September Morn!"

"What's September Morn, Momma?" we had asked. Our question was answered during one of our weekly Saturday library trips. She took us to the Homewood library to see a copy of the painting by a French artist, that of a young nude woman standing in the shallow water of a lake. The painting was titled *September Morn*. When and how did she first learn of this?

Or her partial recitation of Paul Laurence Dunbar's poem "The Party," in which he described a party held on a previous weekend. His descriptions, written and performed in dialect, of both the attendees and the extensive menu could make anyone laugh and salivate at the same time. Two seemingly small examples of what was now becoming an obsession with me. And why now, at eighty years of age, was I obsessed? I soon realized that having reached eighty, I had begun thinking more seriously about my own mortality. I had to face the fact that due to my age and chronic medical problems, it was now time to consider moving out of my home of eighteen years to a more safe and secure environment. After months of laborious conversations and visits to multiple senior care facilities, my wife and I made the decision to move from our home in Santa Monica to a facility in Westwood Village called The Watermark. A facility that has three levels of care: independent living, assisted living, and memory care. Three levels that could care for us even if we were to become increasingly debilitated. We made the decision thoughtfully as we knew that this move would definitely be our last. Once the decision was made, the even more difficult decisions began. We had many questions concerning how to downsize: what to keep, what to sell, what to give and to whom, and the most puzzling question of all, which was why do I have this in the first place?

Keeping that in mind, and being so very aware of my knowledge gaps about my mother's history, I took my wife's suggestion that I first gift as much as possible of my daughters' inheritance to them while I was still alive and also give them an opportunity to fill any gaps in their memories if necessary. This would enable me to not only see and relish their expressions of appreciation and gratitude but also open up an opportunity to ask any unanswered questions they might have.

And so we made the arrangement that Stacey, Nancy Jean, their adopted sister Heather, and I would meet on a Saturday to first go through all of my family picture albums. This gave them all an equal chance to divide the photos between the three of them. The four of us, with their Hawaiian sister on FaceTime, reminisced through many moments of quiet reflection and many more moments of laughter about birthdays, holidays, and ordinary days, with me sometimes being surprised by the accuracy and vividness of their memories.

We could also finally examine and distribute the plethora of antique and contemporary Christmas ornaments we had accumulated over the years. Opening those many dusty boxes, we discovered a riot of brightly colored ornaments: from the antique metallic green bells with flecks of their gray undercoat starting to appear as they aged and the two choirs of candle angels, six white and six black, all dressed in white tops and red gowns, to the bright, sparkling golden set of twelve ornaments from the Danbury Mint, which included a Christmas tree, Santa in his sleigh, and for some reason a Ferris wheel with individual seats that tinkled softly as the wheel turned.

While they had no unanswered questions on this Saturday afternoon, it was clearly understood by all that the opportunity to continue this conversation would always remain open.

After many hours in the dusty garage, our mission for that day, bittersweet as it was, had been accomplished. Physically tired, emotionally stirred, but also relieved, I watched my daughters as they, carrying the last of their treasures of the day, made their way to my elder daughter's car. Nancy Jean playfully tapped the back of her sister's head and Stacey reciprocated by pretending to tickle her. I smiled, as I had seen this same kind of physical interaction between them before. Waving goodbye and closing my front door, I was comforted knowing that all of us would be left with memories of this day and others yet to be experienced and that I, too, still have the opportunity to continue to add to our collective memories before I'm gone.

Goodbye Sue

Chattering like four excited teens, we "girls" piled (albeit not very teen-like) into my sister Judy's car.

The "girls" were Shirley (Snip), seventy-three years old; me, sixty-six; Judy, sixty-four; and Miriam (Mimsi), sixty-one. It had been many years since we four sisters had all been together in Pittsburgh. We had come at this particular time to move our ninety-four-year-old mother from her home to Judy's, an arrangement that everyone felt was long overdue. She had been living alone in the little house on Conemaugh Street, but at ninety-four and with a recent diagnosis of a brain tumor, it was time for a long-term plan.

In our excitement, we had gone straight from the airport to the rehab facility, which was only fifteen minutes from Judy's home. As we entered our mother's room, the air was filled with cries of "Hi Momma!" and "Give me a hug, Momma," along with "I have missed you so much!" With a huge smile on her face, my mother greeted us by gently clasping each of our faces in her hands and then giving us a feather-soft kiss on the forehead. The same way she had greeted us all of our lives. By this time, her speech was unclear because of the tumor, but she managed to mouth each of our names so we knew that she truly recognized each one of us. Although the tumor had been treated with radiation, the doctor had been frank that this was not a cure. Our mother, whom we had always thought of as invincible, had finally met her match, and it looked like the tumor would win.

When we received the news of her diagnosis and prognosis, we discussed whether or not we should be totally honest with her. The radiation would initially bring about some improvement in her symptoms, but that improvement would be short-lived. Subsequent radiation treatments would not be at all effective. Reluctant to share these harsh facts with our mother, we decided not to give her the full prognosis. But mothers, at least our mother, seemed to have an instinctual way of ferreting out the unspoken truth, and the day after we gave our mother an explanation of her prognosis, she and I had a discussion.

"Nancy, did the doctor give all of you the same information that he gave me? Did he tell you anything different? Is there something that you all haven't told me?"

My heart stopped for a minute. How could I tell her the truth, that any additional radiation would not help her? That the tumor would eventually win. Somehow I could not form those words. "No, Momma; we told you everything. The radiation will help some and you won't be fully back to your old self, but you will be better than you are right now."

"Okay, I just wanted to make sure that I had it right, and I knew I could count on you to tell me the truth."

I had a very disturbed evening and night after that conversation. "I knew I could count on you to tell me the truth" kept echoing in my ears. She wanted to know the truth, and we were taking that away from her...which we had no right to do. I knew what I had to do, both for my mother and myself, and I knew I was not going to tell my siblings before I told her. I would tell them afterward. They might be angry, but I couldn't live with myself unless I told her the truth.

I called my mother the next day. With very little preliminary conversation I introduced the subject. "Momma, I want to talk to you about the discussion we had yesterday, because I didn't tell you the whole truth and I'm so sorry."

She said nothing, so I continued and gave her the full explanation. I let her know that we were only trying to protect her, but I realized that this was not fair to her. I repeatedly apologized, cried, and asked for her forgiveness.

Gracious and understanding as always, my mother fully understood what we had tried to do and seemed to appreciate the effort.

"Stop crying, Nancy Jean. Like I said, I knew I could

count on you to tell me the truth, and now I know." After that, the subject seemed to be closed for her, and we had no further conversations about this.

My siblings, in fact, were pleased and relieved when I shared the news with them and admitted to also having misgivings about our initial decision. That evening, while visiting with our mother, we asked her if we could bring her anything special when we visited the next morning. With hand gestures and other means of communicating, we figured out her requested breakfast menu for the next day: bacon, a soft-boiled egg, raisin toast, and "real" coffee. After teasing her about getting fat and another round of feather kisses, we left her, promising to return early the next morning. We stayed up late that night trying to determine how we could best help Judy care for our mother. Judy would still be able to work, as Momma could be alone during the day and had two grandsons to call on if needed. Our mother still received some type of pension from the United Steelworkers union as well as Social Security benefits, and we already knew that one of her neighbor's sons was interested in buying her house so he could be close to his aging father. He had grown up in one of the "row houses" on Conemaugh so he knew all the neighbors in the one long block that made up Conemaugh. Feeling like we were easily making progress, we went to bed feeling very pleased with ourselves.

The next morning we got dressed and were in the midst of preparing my mother's breakfast when the telephone rang. It was the rehab facility calling to tell us that my mother had fallen out of bed during the night but was not injured in any way. The staff did not think she needed to be taken to an ER for evaluation but wanted us to be aware of the incident. We told them we were on our way to visit anyway and would be there shortly. As we were packing up the last of our treats for our mother, the phone rang again. It was the rehab facility telling Judy in a reassuring manner that they had rethought the circumstances of my mother's fall, and while there was still no cause for alarm, they did think she should be examined in Shadyside Hospital. We were instructed to go directly there. The mood in the car was definitely different on this trip. Arriving there, we found our mother lying on a stretcher and only minimally responsive. If we called her "Momma" or "Susie" she responded with only minimal movement of her head. There were no smiles, no feathery kisses, and no signs of recognition. Her doctor of twenty-five years entered the room as we tearfully held each other. He, also tearful, joined us and relayed the information that the only thing keeping her dangerously low blood pressure at its current level was the IV medication she was receiving. He said that we could continue to keep the IV running and have her placed in the ICU. But for how long and to what end? We all agreed that we needed to call our oldest brother and tell him. He said he would immediately take the first flight home and that any decision we made concerning our mother had his blessing.

The next time we saw our mother, we were taken to her room by a member of the palliative care team. Momma was swaddled in blankets from head to toe. She looked very peaceful, like she was resting comfortably. We each took a turn kissing her and saying goodbye. The palliative care nurse promised to notify us of any change in her condition. We left the room not knowing how long our mother would live. It was three in the afternoon. The drive home was short and quiet. What was left to say? We arrived at Judy's home and threw off our jackets, still, I think, in disbelief that everything had changed so much in just three days. The last call came at 3:50 p.m. We knew things would never be the same.

Acceptance

I don't know how long she'd owned it or its origins. It seemed like it had always been there, part of the familiar landscape of our family living room like the TV, the eggshell off-white curtains that framed the large picture window, or the worn caramel-colored sofa with its jumble of pillows of every size, shape, and style. It was certainly present in the last house in which she lived until the year of her death in 2008. My mother had a special place for it on the table that sat beside the comfortable lounge chair where she spent most of her day looking out the window into the neighborhood.

Her morning rituals were prioritized in this way: First, she fixed breakfast for my father. Then she proceeded to make herself a strong cup of coffee lightly laced with Carnation evaporated milk and two spoonfuls of sugar. She would then retire to the living room and settle in her plush easy chair. Before taking even one sip of coffee, she would adjust her little flip calendar. First the month, if needed, then the day of the week, and lastly the date. Only then would she open the newspaper and start her day. After my father's death, her routine changed slightly in that she set a small picture of my father next to the calendar. After a kiss on the picture and "Good morning, Thurston," she would then proceed to the lesser details of changing the date. The calendar wasn't much to look at. In fact, when we were emptying my mother's house after her death, there was no discussion about who got Momma's little flip calendar. No one had any interest in it except me. I wanted something that she loved and that she had physically touched every day. The calendar and a pair of flannel pajamas that I had bought for her, white and adorned with a cascade of red and black blossoms on them, seemed to carry her essence. So I brought those and other mementos back to L.A. with me. That was almost thirteen years ago. The calendar was old even then. Examining it, one noticed the green felt bottom wearing off on two sides of its square metal base. Sitting it upright you could see a small knob on each side of the base that was used to manipulate the contents of an open square next to it. On the left side, the square showed the first three letters of each month. All were neatly typed still, except for the month of October, which had a small tear slightly mutilating the letter C. On the right side were the days of the week typed in the same fashion. Sitting atop the base, the metal continued into the shape of a sphere with a large square cut out in the center which showed the actual date. You turned the left-side knob monthly and changed the day and date daily. Covering both the front and back of the calendar was a map of the world as it was thought to look in the 1800s. Some of the lettering was in French and was accompanied by a picture of a bird and some other creature that looked like it belonged in the sea but was unidentifiable to me. I had always planned to look up the history of a calendar of this type but never did. I will do so now. The calendar found its own spot in my house on the bookshelf right above my desk in what is called my writing room, even though I never write there. It was placed on the same shelf where I keep all my favorite books. My morning ritual was to faithfully flip the calendar to the right date, turn the knob to the day of the week and change the month when necessary.

Mornin' Mamma, I'd think as I touched it. Sometimes I would even say it aloud as I softly kissed it. I loved the feel of the cool smooth metal against my lips as I kissed the faded map. The metal directly under the date was slightly indented after years of her flipping the calendar with her thumb. Ironically, sometimes that particular spot even felt a little warm to me, as if it had just been touched.

This thirteen-year daily ritual was abruptly interrupted by a storm of medical incidents involving Patty. Incidents so severe that it felt like a second pandemic. All thoughts of routine or ritual were replaced by a roller coaster of unpredictable events that occupied every moment of my time. The pandemic continued to rage outside, and crisis after crisis brewed inside the loving, comfortable, serene, mutually supportive, and protective bubble of our home. After weeks of attempting to do the impossible and care for her alone, watching her condition deteriorate with episodic loss of consciousness, decreased mobility, periods of memory loss, and two hospitalizations (including one for the implantation of a pacemaker), I had a total meltdown in the shower one evening. We made the decision to hire a caretaker.

One day after Christmas, after two days of astonishingly poor trial candidates, we found our perfect match. Enrique, a twenty-one-year-old slim, quiet, patient, and always professional Filipino man, made our lives infinitely easier. He worked a fourteen-hour shift seven days a week and unbegrudgingly took on any additional tasks if asked or needed. Enrique slept in my no-writing writing room each night. The same room where the first two caretakers took their breaks and rested during any free time during their shift. After working a month with no off day, Enrique's agency insisted that he be given two days off. Of course, we understood and agreed even though he was totally willing to continue to work without a break. I thought this would give me an opportunity to attack the chaotic mound that was now my desk, and I could also take one small step toward normalcy and bring my beloved calendar, which had been forgotten for some time, into my bedroom. I was especially interested in seeing the date on the calendar—the day when I last thought of rituals and normal, mundane things. I had no idea what that date might be.

I entered the room eagerly and made a beeline to the shelf above my desk and reached for my calendar. No calendar! Wait, of course it had to be there. I was overlooking it. I mean, it was MY calendar! I hurriedly moved the stapler, the staple remover, the little box where I kept paper clips, the flower calendar made by Patty last Christmas, and everything else on that desk. My heart beat faster and my breath became shorter as I moved through the debris. No calendar. It was only after days of frenzied searching, moving furniture, removing every book from the shelves on three walls, and contacting the agency about the whereabouts of the first two caretakers that I would allow myself to believe that it was actually gone.

The five stages of grief, according to Elisabeth Kübler-Ross, are denial, anger, bargaining, depression, and acceptance. At this stage of our lives, all of us have experienced this concept, but until this happened, I had usually thought of it in terms of people as opposed to objects. My thinking has changed.

I found myself dragging through those stages of

grief for a third time feeling like I was pulling a two-ton plow through a massive field of mud. Yes, it was only an object, but to me it was as if a little piece of my heart had been taken from me. I couldn't seem to reach that final stage of acceptance. I'd still awaken in the morning and say good morning to my mother, but somehow it wasn't enough. It was as if the presence of the calendar somehow transported my morning greetings through the universe to my mother and I wanted my damn calendar BACK! Finally, I began looking on eBay for vintage perpetual flip calendars. So many of them. So cheap. None exactly like my mother's but many of the same vintage, with the same type of drawings and spellings. I thought maybe I'd try a new tactic. I'd buy a similar clock and touch it each day as I greeted my mother. Yes, it would be a replacement object and not carry the same meaning, but maybe it would help me feel better.

After a little searching, I did find a calendar on eBay that closely resembled my mother's. Not exactly the same, but close enough for me to take almost a week to consider buying it. But in the end, I did not. I realized that true acceptance did not include a replacement.

Right now, life is slowly returning to some type of new normal for all of us. Fewer Covid cases and deaths. Patty is still on chemo and dialysis, which she has had to accept. She is more mobile, more independent, using a walker, and happily driving. Last weekend, I watched as she walked barefoot on our front lawn, walker pushed aside for the moment but with Enrique close by, as she cut roses for my weekly bouquet. Something she had been unable to do for months. It made my heart sing. Through it all, our bubble, although sorely shaken, has remained securely intact.

Kübler-Ross was right. In the end, it is all about acceptance. And so I awaken each morning, greet my mother and my wife with a good morning and a kiss, and deliver it to them by the best courier available to all of us, which of course is Love.

Nancy McKeever

Nancy at writing retreat

Printed in the USA
CPSIA information can be obtained
www.ICGtesting.com
091215091224
00008B/635